Mahshid Babzartabi

STOP,
Next Chapter

First published by Busybird Publishing 2024

Copyright © 2024 Mahshid Babzartabi

ISBN:
Paperback: 978-1-923216-64-8
Ebook: 978-1-923216-65-5

This work is copyright. Apart from any use permitted under the *Copyright Act 1968*, no part of this publication may be reproduced, stored in a retrieval system or transmitted in any form or by any means, electronic, mechanical, photocopying, recording or otherwise, without the prior written permission of Mahshid Babzartabi.

The information in this book is based on the author's experiences and opinions. The author and publisher disclaim responsibility for any adverse consequences, which may result from use of the information contained herein. Permission to use any external content has been sought by the author. Any breaches will be rectified in further editions of the book.

Cover Image: pexels-quang-nguyen-vinh-222549-2132008

Back cover Images: The cover photos are I and Mahdi in Indonesia, then, and Australia, now.

Cover design: Busybird Publishing

Layout and typesetting: Busybird Publishing

Busybird Publishing
2/118 Para Road
Montmorency, Victoria
Australia 3094
www.busybird.com.au

To all the young people who were executed by the regime including my only hope and love of my life, my son, who departed bravely and courageously.

Also, to all the resilient souls who, despite enduring countless hardships and dangers on the journey to seek refuge, have held on for decades to the fragile thread of hope within the asylum process with determination.

Editor's Foreword

It is an honor to write this foreword for my friend Mahshid, a woman who has become my role model and a living symbol of resilience. Her journey to Australia, filled with unimaginable hardships, is one that many of us can only begin to grasp. She left her homeland in search of freedom, traveling by boat across treacherous seas, facing countless dangers, with nothing but hope in her heart. For ten long years, she lived in limbo, like so many others, caught between the life she fled and the one she dreamed of. Yet, she never stopped fighting for her dream of freedom.

Today as I am writing this foreword, Mahshid stands as one of the 30,000 people who, after a decade of uncertainty, have finally received the gift of permanency in Australia. Her strength is a testament to the human spirit's will to survive and thrive, even when the odds are stacked against it.

But while her story has reached this moment of relief, there are still thousands of asylum seekers who remain in limbo—people who risked everything, who accepted any danger, just to have a chance at the life we often take for granted. They continue to wait, patiently and hopeful, yearning for the same freedom that my friend has now secured.

Let us hope that Australia, a country built on the promise of opportunity and refuge, will handle this chapter of its history with compassion. May we not look back one day with the need to apologize once more to those who sought nothing more than safety and a new start on our shores. Instead, let us work together to ensure that the future is one where no one must flee in fear, and where the brave sacrifices of asylum seekers are met with dignity and justice.

Rana Ebrahimi

Chapter 1

Her words, filled with harshness and demands, paraded before my eyes, growing uglier with each repetition. A strange sense of dizziness enveloped me. Gradually, her voice became distant, fading into oblivion as if I had lost both my hearing and sight. All that remained was the relentless onslaught of her harsh, disorderly, and insistent words, searing my weary and disappointed nerves, already frayed from past trauma. But today, I had even stronger reasons to fall apart.

Perhaps in such an all-too-familiar situation, the wisest thing to do would be to give up once more, followed by yet another experience of failure. The weight of the word "fail" burdened my heart, tempting me to abandon all hope. Maybe it was time to let go of my aspirations for this job, for the publication of this book, and give up on this career altogether. This is not a job one could overcome without being one of them and a part of their corrupt system.

Her harsh words served as a reminder that as long as I wasn't one of them, as long as I refused to turn a blind eye to their actions and refused to glorify those in power, my translations and whatever I wrote would forever be draped in an unsightly garment of censorship, favoring their interests. The only way for someone in my situation to climb the ladder of dreams was to do what I always hated—flatter those in power, become their virtual slave in any way possible. But I can't live with myself if I obey this unwritten rule of prosperity in this land that I love most. Yet the reality is crystal clear—there is no other way but their way if you want a bright future or, more importantly, a safe life.

When will it be my turn in life? I have been waiting and dreaming of this for many years. The answer is also crystal clear. I can see and feel it even more clearly now—NEVER. In this corrupt and stagnant environment, there is never a chance for people like me. I had glimpsed this truth before, stupidly holding on to false hopes that one day someone among them would exhibit a glimmer of fairness and humanity.

But in a system tainted by corruption, this hope was mere illusion, especially for someone like me—an ordinary individual without any political connections. When I was younger, it was easier to dream and grow false hope that one day someone among them would act differently, care more about facts and talents rather than connections. Today, I am either old enough not to believe in such dreams or wise enough to live in reality, to open my eyes to what is in front of me and its bitter consequences.

This not-so-new experience reminded me of something I once heard from an old, wise man: the world belongs to the beautiful and wealthy. For the rest of us, there is nothing further in life; we simply came into this world to keep the stadium crowded. I have been part of the crowd long enough. And I think in countries like Iran, where the entire political system is run by corruption. No matter how hard you try, how educated or talented you are, without any connection with those above in this system, you are lost in the crowd. It has been proven to me over and over, many times.

Even when I was so desperate to improve my job level, I tried to connect with the system somehow, but the ugly and cruel gestures of it made me hate myself even more.

No, this does not work for me in any way possible. I'm not the one who can match this corrupt system. Even if I force myself to do so, I will hate myself so much that I wouldn't be able to live in peace.

So, what's the solution? Maybe nothing. Or I should say, what is left for people like me at the end of the day is only disappointment. It doesn't matter how diligently I work or how passionate I am about my field of education, or how talented I prove to be—the only way that works for you is blindly being connected to the system. In countries like Iran, the final outcomes always hinge on political connections and affiliations, dictating the opportunities available to individuals. The only path to success is through these connections, at the expense of growth and advancement for those without such privileges. They stole my dignity and murdered all my hopes.

Although I could go on in the same situation, I can't anymore, as I've lost hope for any bright future for myself in this homeland—a home that treats me as a stranger. But where could I go at the age of 52? Where in the world could possibly offer any chances for a woman my age to start from scratch? And even if such a place exists, how am I able to cope with all the physical and financial limitations I must confront? Which door in this whole wide world is open for me?

Black clouds of dark thoughts hover over my mind, questions one after another, all carrying heavy, unbearable pieces of disappointment within my tired, heavy head.

The only solace I could find in this situation was a bitter smile. At least this time, my translated book had not been stolen as had happened with my previous two works. However, even if my work remained intact, another unjust process had taken place, as was customary in every field of activity within Iran. We could see such in every other field of life in Iran, and we were so familiar with it that as soon as we faced it, we knew where the source was.

Every word of my work, or any other book, I must say, was murdered under the sharp, ugly, and merciless censorship wielded by those in power, who had no qualms about stifling any talent that challenged their interests. And such a catastrophe is not just planned for books but all sorts of arts and so on.

"Why are you complaining instead of being grateful that your translated book is being published?" continued the voice; "Not everybody has the chance that you have now, and you know it very well. But instead of being grateful and finishing what you're here for, you keep complaining and playing innocent." It seemed her ugly words, sourced from her chicken-sized mind, would never end. Her injected lips parted to form these words. Her heavily tattooed eyebrow made her as ugly as her words. This was the pinnacle of sympathy she could offer, but every aspect of her countenance, just like her false empathy, was as fake as could be.

Her fake lips unleashed a cascade of diplomatic words: "You must understand the country you reside in—an Islamic ruling country. Such rules naturally restrict the freedom to use certain sentences and words in your so-called translation. But it looks like you absolutely have no idea where you are living, do you?" She opened her eyes wide in a sign of wonder or maybe a threat. With that ugly smile, one eyebrow raised, and a smart, staring look, she continued, her fake confidence based on her corrupt relationships allowing her to mock me as much as she needed to fulfill her complexity in her uglier attitude.

"I am not the writer of the book; I am merely its translator. And I believe that accepting and allowing its publication with the main parts censored is a betrayal to both the book and its contents, to its writer, and to our profession. Even if you argue that censoring certain parts will not harm the overall concept, I strongly disagree with this extensive censorship," I replied, my voice laden with frustration and disappointment, apparent to anyone who listened—anyone but this head-to-toe fake lady who deliberately tried to play deaf, which really suited her considering her rude behavior.

This blatant disregard for the principles that lend value to translation was crystal clear proof. Yet, like everyone else in her position, encompassed within a corrupt system in every moment of their life, she had made her decision to feign ignorance, distancing herself from any semblance of reality or truth, which worked best for her and her dirty position. Especially when it came from someone like me, who lacked connections to those in power and had no strength to climb over this hierarchy—someone who did not belong to their inner circle, someone who was not part of their mafia, didn't want to be, or even had any willingness to pretend.

Although her lips were closed now, waiting for my confirmation as she was used to, I could still hear the loud "get lost" finished by just looking at her cold but happy eyes—happy from mocking me. I knew that looked very good. I fixed another one of those cheeky rebellions to teach her who the boss was. But she knew very well people like me would never have enough talent to join her scenario, and perhaps that was why she threw her arrows of blaming and harsh words even harder at me. There was not even one single word that could bring connections between both of our ideas and beliefs. There was no use continuing this erupting conversation. It was better to leave; maybe later I would be able to find a way or someone to help me with this. An alternative I knew wouldn't work the moment it came to my mind, but it was better to stay on that never-ending humiliation.

As I was on my way out of her office, the weight of my feet felt like the heaviest burden in the world, surpassing even the crushing blow to my shattered and bruised spirit inflicted by her words. The best favor I could do for myself in such a scene was to carry my entire being, striving to escape from that suffocating atmosphere and run out with no further words.

Once again, it happened. I knew what I should do as this familiar heaviness settled upon me before. Yes, it was not entirely unfamiliar, as I had experienced this bitterness before, particularly when the issue concerned my previous book. And now, yet again, I gathered the shattered fragments of my pride, attempting to find solace in the fact that at the very least, my book had not been stolen to serve someone else's agenda as had befallen me in my previous encounters with such individuals.

Although this did not even help me gain more comfort in these harsh moments, it was a way to ease the heaviness I was feeling in my body and soul, both desperately needing to fool myself somehow. I needed even a very tiny positive fact to distract my mind and soul, both, and postpone that heaviness to sometime later, even if by later I mean a few hours later.

However, even if I managed to convince myself of this consolation, trying hard to give myself a bit of comfort, it was incapable of dulling the sharp pain of being bullied once more. Although, as a woman, I should have gotten used to being bullied—it's not a new sense. It's a sense we women who grow up in countries like Iran are always very familiar with. Yes, it's common sense for all women who live in Eastern-style countries. It's part of our daily life, and we are almost born with this feeling of being bullied as a normal part of daily life.

The level of harshness may vary each time, but it's happening every day and everywhere, and for every other woman with different scenes as well. It's so common in most cases one might get so used to it or not even feel it. But I still feel it strongly, and the pain emanates from the harsh reality that there is no chance for individuals like me to thrive in this environment.

My first and most important unforgivable sin is that I am a woman, and an even bigger sin is that I couldn't—or I must say, didn't want to—become one of them. Unfortunately, I couldn't confront them either, as they were too powerful and still are. The entire nation, for nearly four decades, has failed to confront this corrupt system ruling the country and its mafia-like presence. What happens if you do? Although it's clear, I'll tell you: what happens if you confront the corrupt system? As an individual, I would only find myself trapped within their horrific prisons, subjected to unimaginable torture—a fate awaiting anyone who dares to stand against them in any way possible.

If you are not one of them, or if you don't obey and accept their possession over your life, mind, and soul; if you are not lucky enough to be attached to any connection or affiliation, you would forever wander within the vicious circle they have designed for people like us until the end of our days. For those who are looking at the subject from the outside, it might seem like an exaggeration, but the whole story in reality is even worse. Witnesses to these words are all these young and innocent people who are being massacred just because they are fighting for their basic human rights.

I reflected on the countless days and nights I had dedicated to translating this book, nurturing hopes and dreams that it would finally bear my name as the published translator. It was a pivotal milestone in my years of work in this field, opening the doors for future translations and writings, which were not only my true passion but also a tool to open doors for more jobs. Oh, what a delusion it was for someone without political connections! It was an unattainable feat; I could be certain it would never transpire. These were the words my broken heart incessantly echoed within my heavy, tired mind.

Walking toward the bus station with these thoughts swirling within me, I could almost hear the cacophony of broken pieces colliding—a symphony of shattered dreams relentlessly repeating, "Don't deceive yourself; it will never work—especially as long as you hold onto the hope that one of these people will ever swim against their own interests and favors, suddenly transform, and support individuals like you." What a fool I was to believe this would ever happen. None of them will ever take your side, as their survival depends on supporting each other, not others.

As I sank into the bus seat, I surrendered all those fragmented, clamoring pieces of myself into the embrace of an imaginary, compassionate family member—an individual who would hold them tightly, unafraid of their sharp edges, someone capable of providing solace in these cruel moments, softly whispering, "Everything will be okay, don't worry. It's not the end of the world; we will fix it together." Together with whom? No, I do not have anyone to wash away all the sorrow and stress I am experiencing at the moment.

The bus seat, in its silent companionship, assumed the role of the sympathetic friend I desperately needed in that moment. Yet the reality was stark—there was no one. No one present in that bus seat or anywhere else except for me. There was no one waiting even at home or anywhere else to offer comforting words. I yearned to hear words of support, but there was no caring family member to utter them. Instead, all that awaited me at home were accusing eyes and a scowl of disapproval, ready to place the blame squarely on my shoulders. I wished I had somewhere else to seek refuge, but home—bitter home—was the only option now.

Again, heavy thoughts wouldn't leave my head for even one minute. In a forceful, corrupt system that subjects its people to immense pressure and cruelty, only expecting obedience from the masses, it is widely understood that one cannot fight or stand against this corrupt system alone. Individuals are well aware of the consequences they will face if they swim against the current of this strong river. In such cases, it becomes easier to shift blame onto the closest person within reach. And this time, that person was me—at least in my home, it was like this.

"You have no idea where you live," how familiar those words sounded. "You lack the understanding of the system that operates in this country. Why can't you learn to compromise a little, to align yourself with those in power? The only path to success here is becoming one of them. Can't you see it? You can't, you can't, you can't." How familiar I was with all these cruel words and unfair judgments from someone who never missed an opportunity to remind me how incapable I am.

Yes, these were the words that awaited me at home, likely harsher than before, as it was not the first time. The blame had to be stronger this time, penetrating the depths of my empty mind more effectively—or so he believed. I had heard these words countless times before, every time I sought to find fulfillment, to prove my worth as a human being, not just as a woman and not as a second-class citizen that I always hated being. In some cases, not even second-class but relegated to the lowest rung of society.

At the age of 52, having already endured the loss of one child in the most devastating circumstances at the hand of this regime's men and witnessing another son trapped in an equally distressing situation (today, as I write this, my other son is in heaven too), I found myself in a state of helplessness, unable to assist my own flesh and blood. I lacked immediate family members I could rely on or find consolation in, except for a constantly accusing husband who blamed me for failing to fit into the corrupt system. Practically, he didn't care how well I fit with the system; what he cared about was if there was no success in publishing my book, there would be no more money from me. That was the sad, real part of the story, and we both knew it very well, though I was scared to admit it to myself—that my only value in the house was how I could increase the income spent in this house and nothing else. As bad luck would have it, this was the extent of sympathy I experienced in such circumstances, and honestly, I could not expect more.

To tell the truth, in fact, this reaction was one that any woman could expect from a forceful, corrupt, male-dominated system, more or less. I am not the only victim of a male-dominated society, but this time I was too tired to get over it and bottle up, as we are usually trained to do.

"You are a woman, and that is enough. So it's always your fault in any situation where things go wrong. No one else gets blamed except females—in any family, oh no, not just in the family, but in the whole society. Contrary to Saudi Arabia, you might say women have more freedom. Yes, they do; for example, they have permission to drive in Iran, but they face being bullied on the road every day. Such prejudicial attitudes have caused more life-threatening accidents for women daily since they cannot fully concentrate on driving abilities and must be more careful about both their driving and being bullied by those men in society who are against the fact that they can drive as well as men. And at the end of the day, how it's interpreted is that women are no good for driving on the road compared to men.

Constant disappointment loomed over every endeavor, whether pursued out of passion or as a profession, for a woman like me who refused to confine herself to the endless dictates of her male counterparts. Translating and writing were not mere jobs for me; they provided a sanctuary, a respite from the stresses of daily life.

But how could I consider this work true translation if someone or some system dictated what I could and couldn't write? To bow down to such censorship would be a betrayal to the book, to my profession, and even more broadly, to all translators in the world. It undermined the purpose of translation, which was to convey the writer's true message to the community, not to align with the interests of a select few.

As a translator, my duty was to faithfully interpret the author's words and ideas to ensure the real message was conveyed. Translation was not just a means to support myself financially or to showcase my educational qualifications, though I always enjoyed every single moment spent on this job. But every translator has a mission to accomplish, and it's not just based on words and correct vocabulary. If I failed to deliver the writer's authentic message, I would jeopardize my reputation as a translator and my integrity as a human being.

Translating is my refuge, my sanctuary, where I find the peace I crave. Whenever I sit down to work, I immerse myself in each word and sentence I translate, letting go of the outside world. This practice brings me the desired relief and tranquility. I believe others can relate, as we all have our own sacred havens to escape the chaos of life.

Maybe it's not a perfect comparison, but for me, it's like the moments I spend cooking in the kitchen or the time when I used to prepare meals for my children, eagerly awaiting their return from school. It was not just about fulfilling my parenting duty or even the joy of serving my family; it was my moment of 'me.' Translation held the same significance for me. As a woman living in the harsh atmosphere of a country like Iran, you need to create your own sanctuary to seek refuge in, and for me, that was the real meaning my job had for me.

Although, comparing cooking and translating may not be the perfect analogy, both activities yield the same comforting and relaxing results—at least for me.

As an Iranian woman of my generation, I was raised to be an obedient wife, constantly on duty, although I didn't learn my lesson properly as parents and society expected me to do. Since childhood, I've been taught by my parents, family members, traditions, and society about how a good woman should act in front of her father, brother, and husband. The whole idea was to mold females into believing that their purpose was to be a source of comfort and pleasure for men—a docile figure that conforms to their desires, although I always hated it and, deep down, never believed in it, always trying somehow to escape from these false old beliefs. As a woman in such a society, I was expected to act like a robot, always following their orders.

These men, whether they be fathers, brothers, husbands, or even sons, held our (women in such society) lives, minds, and destinies in their hands. The narrative of our lives was written by them, and the most crucial aspect of our existence was to ensure their happiness and satisfaction. Above all, we were expected to say one word in their presence: YES. And nothing else was accepted from a woman, otherwise, she was considered to be rebellious. We were made to forget our own humanity, our share in life, and finally, to forget our own existence. Did we even have any other choice? Sadly, no.

What do they call a woman who dares to stand against this lined pattern for women's lives? Or, in this atmosphere, a woman who says no to decisions made for her, even before her existence? Definitely, she should be fade away from life's page,, or she and her disobedient attitude will contaminate all other women's minds—something exactly like what is happening today in Iran. But what we see today in Iran's recent uprising are women getting stronger and stronger despite what they think is a faded woman. These women are from a younger generation who are not afraid of anything—neither men nor the corrupt system—a system designed to take away all their dignity and educate the community to be robots just in their favor. That plan never works well. Sooner or later, the system will break down; history has proven this in many other cases. They are free to call these women rebellious or any dirty name they wish, but the reality is that each time these women are fighting stronger than before for their basic human rights, and the whole world is going to be on their side soon.

But back then, for women of my generation, the story was different, especially because the majority of women were illiterate or had only elementary education. Then, sadly, it was totally different from what we are witnessing now. We did not have freedom of choice, even in minor matters of our own lives, like what to wear, where to go, or even what to read. As women, our sole purpose was to conform to society's limited definition of a "good woman" that these men held in their minds.

Over time, these notions became deeply ingrained, and most women accepted their roles as second-class citizens, often even lower—maybe they didn't feel strong enough to stand and fight constantly. They accepted temporary peace like how birds accept cages for enough food. Although it is promising to note that younger generations of women face fewer constraints and forced traditions, that is the main reason why the Mahsa revolution got the chance and possibility to happen—because the younger generation dares to talk and fight for their rights. The field for this huge revolutionary change was prepared through education and increased awareness, especially by media.

They are fighting for their rights as human beings, and they are not scared, although the same story of death and torture is still strongly, even more strongly than before, in place. This progress marks a significant improvement in the lives of women in countries like mine, although they are paying a high price for it. But it's worth it.

These women, who are mostly young girls, tirelessly, endlessly, and above all, bravely continue on this uprising till the end, and the world will witness a better Iran, not so far from what it is now. This wave of freedom is ongoing; once started, it can't be stopped. They might be able to prevent the progress of the current situation by resorting to force and intimidation for a while, but they will never be able to extinguish this fire, which is fueled by the bloodshed the regime started itself.

Back to women's rights in countries like Iran—even throughout history and across generations this narrative of men controlling society has been repeated relentlessly, and many women have accepted these unwritten rules with every fiber of their being, accepting their status as perpetual victims. To be honest, I think some even enjoyed it as it would give them less responsibility.

But for some, it's so believed that it's like the word of a Bible, which actually in some matters it is, since the whole country is managed and based on religious orders, and one of the main Islamic religious orders is obeying totally, without any question, from the men of the house, blindly. These types of women have believed that challenging these norms is an unforgivable sin, a violation of the false comfort zone they have come to accept. These women have been deliberately brainwashed to believe that a woman who fights for her rights will be eternally condemned.

Unfortunately, even in the face of progress, the system still favors men, especially in legal and judicial matters. Severe disparities persist, such as a woman's inability to travel abroad without the permission of her father or husband. In tragic accidents, the compensation offered to a woman's family is often a fraction of what would be paid for the damage to a man's body. When it comes to divorce and child custody, a mother's rights are significantly limited unless she obtains the father's consent. Numerous unbelievable, cruel, and I must say barbaric rules, nonsense obligations, and practices underscore the devaluation of women as human beings in comparison to their counterparts in Western societies.

For me, given the immense power of this entrenched system, my story takes a different turn. Many women believed that by voicing their objections, they could eventually reclaim their rights. However, their efforts only led to years of torment in prisons, and that is just the end for those who are lucky. Others with less luck, and those who are considered to be more rebellious, will be executed without any questions, even for their relatives and immediate family members. And that is no joke at all, as we are now witnessing every day, with the nonstop executions of young men and women in prisons. Not only did I not want either of these fates for myself, but I didn't want to isolate myself at home either.

On the other hand, I truly had no idea how many more years I would have to endure under this system. At 52 years old, I've lost all opportunities to experience the simple joys of being treated as a human being due to these suffocating traditions and policies ruling the country. The current corrupt government further exacerbates the challenges faced by women, making it even more difficult for those who dare to confront their fears and resist this system in any way possible. Unfortunately, society often views and accepts such resistance as a form of anti-woman sentiment, due to the same old beliefs and concepts of what is known as a "good woman" in the eyes of old-fashioned minds.

I cannot bear to live like this until the end of my days—I have been patient enough, even more than enough so far. I have made up my mind to leave this country by any means possible, and I plan for it to happen very soon, without wasting any more time. Maybe I was not courageous enough before, and as I get closer to the end of my time, I not only dare, but also feel there is no other solution. Even though before I was more inclined to fantasize that things might get better, each passing day brings further deterioration, and I've witnessed the worsening conditions over the past 40 years since the revolution. I see no bright future in this hell. I am not sure whether there is a heaven out there for me or not, but I cannot sit in this hell and do nothing, waiting for any possible change. It's surely, definitely, and absolutely a no—not anymore.

It is time to make the final decision for my life, no matter how scared I am to follow this decision. I have no choice but to overcome this fear; otherwise, I am condemned to continue the same lifestyle and be buried under the heavy burden of this life, gradually and deeply drowning in the same old pattern I always hated the most. It's not just because I do not like these patterns for my life; I cannot live life the same once an awakening has happened. I cannot pretend it's not there and still pretend to be asleep when I know I am not. Otherwise, not only would putting up with the system be impossible, but I wouldn't even be able to live with myself.

It might seem like an excuse, but I am blaming the corrupt system for my failure now. Then, I would always have to blame myself and no one else. The thought struck me while sitting on the bus heading back home. Continuing serves no purpose. I will leave, and that will be it. Staying here only means enduring the same cycle, each time in a different shape and with different words, but always resulting in disappointment and nothing else. Or staying might result in an even worse scenario in the future—if I dare to stand clearly and raise my voice for society to hear me, jail and torture would be waiting for me, as it happened to many who bravely did not choose to stay silent before me.

It hits me harder with each occurrence, and it's the last thing I ever wanted to happen to me. However, now it seems to be the wisest decision, at least from my current point of view now that I have lost hope for the change I used to believe in. Contemplating leaving while my shattered sense of pride clashed violently within me brought about a deafening crash, reverberating through my weary body. I could almost hear the painful echo and feel it consuming the last remaining traces of energy from my broken body.

YES, that would be the next step and the last one in this homeland—a home that is far more a stranger than any unknown land. But is there any promised land in the world? I do not know. It probably depends on my interpretation of a promised land. The only interpretation I have in my mind now is a place where I can feel safe enough to be myself, a place where I can dare to open the NEXT CHAPTER of my life. Otherwise, this book of my life is better closed—nothing more in further chapters for me as its sole reader.

Chapter Two

The mere thought that on the other side of the world there might be a glimmer of hope for people like me—hopes that could revitalize me, giving me a sliver of renewed energy to write freely—now, at this moment, I can't even hold a pen in my hands or even look at it on my computer screenscreen. I desperately need that freedom taken away from me by authorities.

What I am facing right now makes me feel like running away from any sort of writing. It is now, for me, the hardest job ever done in my life. If I try to find a new survival in a new place, a place far from unlawful bans and restrictions on writing, perhaps I can finally pursue my passion and prove to myself—solely to myself—that finally, for the first time in my life, it is possible to call myself a free woman.

The empty heads of these people make it so hard for them to understand someone like me, who lacks any government connections, substantial wealth, and above all, is not on the same page with them, as I resolutely persevere and support my beliefs and actions within society. Yes, I need to prove it to myself, or perhaps to them too, that I am not just a woman, even though in their eyes it's the only interpretation they can have of my existence. I owe it not only to myself but to every woman in the same or similar situation. I must prove that I am a human being and also the fact that as long as I can breathe, I can still pursue my passion and follow my dreams.

Although I already have a good income from this job, I am not wealthy enough to migrate overseas in any other situation than as a refugee. On the other hand, any form of migration is a long-term process with fewer chances considering my age limitations. For many destination countries to accept you as a refugee, your life must be in great danger and in a life-threatening situation. For me, it's not that my life is in immediate danger here, but my dignity, identity, and entire being have been irreparably damaged, which perhaps are not good reasons to get my hands on a migration visa. Although I cannot consider myself a protected, dignified human being in this country, continuing here would mean I have to stand against the system, and then it would definitely be a life-threatening situation for me when it's definitely too late for everything.

Aligning myself with this system and walking its path is something I, as an individual, cannot easily embrace. It goes against everything I have learned so far and taught my children. If I could convince myself to be part of it, nowhere else in the world would be better for me than here. But throughout my life, I have always stood and acted against corruption in any way possible. So far, I have not been a rebel, but it will end up in this pattern too, as it's really impossible for someone like me to walk any other path than this.

I yearn to be able to live in peace with myself, and that is simply impossible in this country. For those whose peace relies on freedom from the filthiness, corruption, and dependency on a flawed system, I must say my current situation is not how I define peace in my life.

All the arguments surrounding this momentous decision were predictable, but I didn't want to proceed with arguments. No, that wouldn't be the right approach. What I needed was to act peacefully and, at least this time, act very politically. Any other method would not bring me closer to what I desired and needed to do. I yearned for a life of freedom and self-expression. To achieve that, I must depart from this unpromising land and find a place where I can be recognized and treated as a human being—a human being who simply wants to stand on her own feet, relying on her own abilities and preserving whatever remains of her dignity. It might seem like I am repeating this new idea, which truly is not very new, but that is the only thing giving me comfort in my head for now.

But I need to start wisely with every new step. If I were to begin with arguments, my perpetually disagreeing husband could easily prevent me from traveling overseas. His power over me is not only for traveling that you need the man of the house's permission. In the case of any even emergency health issues, when you need or want to have any surgery on your own body, you cannot get it done without their permission. It doesn't matter how bad your health situation is, even if it is life-threatening.

These unfair, illogical regulations always work in favor of male citizens. You do not have any authority over your own body or health, nor any rights to plan and control your life, but they do. It might seem unbelievable to women who live in Western-style countries, but this is only one of the thousands of injustices and cruel Islamic rules about women in Iran. Back to the process of leaving the country, I realized that I must act gently when talking to my husband to convince him to sign the letter of consent for me. Without this letter of consent from him, every other attempt will be useless.

According to current legal law, every woman must provide this letter to authorities by the time she is leaving the country under any circumstances, and this law is not changeable for any reason. Any other route would be impossible for me to achieve my goal, and that's when my decision would definitely come to a halt. Yes, that is very possible—he has the authority, and he will definitely use it if I don't do what he wants or what he wishes too. He is a man, and every court would grant him the authority to obstruct anything I wish to do with my life.

Islamic regulations dictate that a woman's permission to travel or leave the country must come solely from her husband's consent, and that's for married women. For single women who have not had any marriage history, it's their father who makes the final decision unless they are above a certain age, like 40. Such laws have nothing to do with a woman's own will or consent. She is rendered powerless when making the most significant decisions in her life.

All these unbelievable, barbaric bans for women are the reality of our lives. Insulting rules of when a woman desires to marry for the first time, she can only do so with her father's permission. You may now better understand the letter of consent I mentioned—it's always, in all situations of your life, about a man's consent or a man's will. And similarly, the worst is that this law won't change, no matter what evidence you offer to prove it's necessary for travel or even surgery. Only the highest legal chief commander can cancel this law with a formal certificate signed and sealed by himself. But from what I have told you so far, do you think any ordinary citizen could reach him to ask for such a favor?

There are thousands of medical files of women who needed surgery, and their husbands found the procedure not in their favor or just by their own judgment—not based on medical or scientific evidence—though it was not appropriate for their wife. Eventually, many of these women lost their lives because their husbands did not sign the letter of consent. This is exactly what should be called a silent and legal murder. It is always a man who makes final decisions for women, determining what they should or should not do. It is always a man who paints the canvas of their future and destiny. Even if a woman decides not to have children whatsoever, she again requires her man's consent to make it possible. If a woman, for any reason, decides to end her pregnancy, even legally or for any other reason, and she does it by her own will without her husband's letter of consent, she will be labeled as a murderer of her own child and legally prosecuted.

Who is a woman in countries like this? She is nobody with regard to her own rights, choices, and decisions—rights that are accepted everywhere else in the world where a woman is valued as a human and is not judged by her sex. That is how it should be everywhere, rather than in most countries with Islamic rules. No, not anymore—what else could I do other than live free with the only life I have?

One thing I know about myself for sure: I do not want to become a victim of this country's patriarchy and traditions anymore. Enough is enough for me—in fact, even now, it's too late. I shouldn't have put up with all these bans all these years and had false hope that soon a better life would happen. I must seize any opportunity available to break free from this suffocating environment. He, my husband, who has the authority over my life according to law, could effortlessly ban me from leaving the country, and according to the current family laws, he had every right to do so. I knew it all my life, but part of this passion came from fear, which has faded for the moment, and that fear led me to a false hope that change would come somehow from some unknown source, just like in fairy tales.

I am too old now to believe in such fairy tales anymore, and too hopeless with not much time to waste on these kinds of childish, fake hopes. Otherwise, there is only one end waiting for me, and that is that I would have to sit and watch my dreams of pursuing my passion be shattered. I knew for sure if I just went home and honestly told him what I had in my mind—whatever is in my mind brought to my mouth for a case God forbid—and stupidly think, as a human, I have the right to live free and pursue my dreams, definitely, from the very first moment I open my mouth, I must bury those dreams. I didn't need to convince him with logical explanations; it wouldn't work, and I was sure about it. No, it never works in my favor. But the wisest action was to deceive him in any way possible—that's what would let me get what I really want more than anything else at the moment, and that is to leave this circle of bans and walls I have been trapped in all my life. Time to break these walls at any cost, even at the cost of my life—that's the final decision and solution for me.

Although that was not my ideal plan either, it was the only way that could work in such a case. Looking at the whole story, it was not even deceiving him but giving him what he cared about more than my presence in his life—and that was only money. I have lived with him long enough to know this bitter reality very well. I knew him all too well. I knew that to tempt him, I had to grant him power of attorney over everything I had tirelessly worked for over the past two decades. Even though it was crystal clear to me that I would lose everything I had sweated day and night to attain, this was the price I had to pay_the only way left for me if I wanted to taste freedom and the feeling of being respected for my own choices and decisions at some point in my life.

While I was preparing and devising ways to convince my husband to accept my decision, I also conducted some research to determine the fastest and perhaps safest way to achieve this long-held goal of mine—if such a safe route even existed. But the first and most challenging step in this scenario was obtaining his consent, and that for sure wouldn't be easy or even close. As the Persian saying goes, while I was cooking up my plans for him in my mind, I was conducting my research for the best way to get out too.

Simultaneously, I reached out to my cousins in Europe, asking them to send me an invitation letter to set foot on the initial stage of my journey. Obtaining a visa from one of the European countries shouldn't be difficult since I had previously traveled to Europe several times as a commercial interpreter. However, this time I knew I never wanted to return to this perpetual open-wall prison. This time it would be a different story. I also had to be honest with them and let them know that this time I am planning to stay and never want to come back again. I did not have to go through all the details except the main thing, which is staying and not planning to come back to this hell again—maybe that would lead to never, who knows—but definitely not as long as this government is ruling when women are considered to be nothing but a toy in men's hands.

If I were to clearly state during my visa interview that I intended to stay permanently and never come back, I would never be granted a visa in my passport. Therefore, I needed to be at least honest with my cousin, who was going to be my sponsor in the visa process. He deserved to know. I didn't want my family to face any potential hardships for my sake—that wouldn't be fair to them. He had a thriving business in Germany, and he had worked diligently for over 30 years to establish it. Taking advantage of his trust and making him my sponsor would constitute a betrayal of his trust, which would deeply hurt him and myself as well. For me, building my dream of freedom on the foundation of betraying someone else was out of the question.

However, when I informed him that I intended to come and stay permanently this time upon arriving in Europe, he simply refused to send me an invitation letter. My cousin told me that if he sent me an invitation and I came to stay, he and his business would be in trouble. This was exactly what I had expected to hear from him, and I didn't want him and his family to face any difficulty based on my situation. Besides, I was leaving this country to live freely and rely on myself, not someone else. It would be a great help if he was still willing to help me, but it's very much understandable that his own life, his family, and his business come first. If I were to hide my intention from him, I would definitely lose all sorts of support as well, including his trust forever. No matter how much support you have or how great your financial situation is, in at least the first few months of migration, even in very normal ways, you definitely need a great deal of support. Without his consent to this, how could I be sure of him giving me the support I needed? It's not merely financial support but perhaps any social or emotional support—maybe even more important. Besides, this was a country I had zero knowledge of in terms of its common language. No language, not a great amount of cash, no support from anyone—what would be left for me in this unknown destination? No, this option is so far a big NO.

Although that was very understandable for me, it left me feeling stressed and confused about how this could possibly happen. There was only one window of hope open, and now it's totally closed. Other options were not much more reachable either. Obviously, there are other options too, like applying for other sorts of migration visas, but all other options were long-term and very expensive processes, which I was not sure I would be able to handle either way. And also, considering my age, there was not much hope for me, even if I had all the other required criteria—my age range would ruin them all.

The only profession I had all my life was translating, writing, and so on, but I learned it through experience, not based on an academic level. For a skilled visa, you need lots of long-term paperwork and also an academic degree, and at the end of the day, there is no guarantee that your application will pass all those terms and conditions and that you will be able to get your hands on a skilled visa. And it was the same with all other sorts of visa issuing processes, at least for me and in my conditions.

I truly want to leave behind all the restrictions and uncertainties in life. At this moment, I don't want anything more, and I can't think of anything else. It's as if my brain is frozen in all other areas, and only this part is functioning now. Every day, it becomes increasingly impossible to bear this constant, unclear future. One thing I am absolutely certain about, with zero doubt, is that I must go. But where?

Europe now seems like an impossible destination. Not only because of the cold response I received from my cousin but also due to the language barrier, which would hinder any future progress. After all, that's the main reason behind my strange idea of migrating. Even if I took a chance and hit the road, choosing any European country as my final destination, a bigger problem arises: I wouldn't be able to communicate in society.

Language is one of the most important factors in a successful migration. It might not seem critical to some, and they might go ahead without thinking about the future, but for me, as an interpreter, it's crucial. I know very well that without language skills, it's better to stay put and dismiss the idea of migration. There won't be any bright future there for me either.

I want to leave this homeland because I want to be active in society. But how could that be possible for someone who cannot speak the language and engage in societal affairs? No, both migration and freedom are important to me, but I also want to be involved in society, as I have been for most of my life. I don't want to just sit at home, doing nothing. If that were the case, I could stay here, remain inactive, and continue living a remote lifestyle. At least I would be safe in my comfort zone—safe, like a prisoner in a jail.

I needed a letter of invitation, and suddenly, a new idea came to mind: asking one of the companies I had worked with as an interpreter in the past. However, I would have to tell them the truth, and once they found out about my plan, they would definitely refuse to send the invitation letter. My own family didn't support me when they learned the truth; what could I expect from people I've only met briefly in business meetings? To be honest, I expect no one to help me with this issue. Although I needed the letter badly, I've learned through all the hard situations in my life that I can rely on no one but myself. This reality is a bit scary and disappointing, but it's the truth of my whole life, and sadly, this situation is no different.

Chapter Three

I kept trying to encourage myself, repeating, "Don't get disappointed. There's always another way." Not everyone who left the country before you had relatives to support them or a lot of money, but deep down, a swarm of anxious butterflies fluttered wildly in my stomach.

It was as if a wise mother was advising my troubled soul, telling me to stay calm, be patient, and think of a Plan B. I began searching for different ways to escape this constant nightmare. A friend mentioned that one of her relatives had decided to leave the country forever under similar circumstances and planned to go to Australia by boat. "By boat?!" How could that be? Is it really possible to sail such a long distance? Australia is so far away, surrounded by the sea on all sides. It seemed unimaginable, but maybe it was worth at least researching.

My mind immediately conjured images from movies—people lost at sea, landing on isolated shores, or worse, ending up in the hands of devil people or drowning in the ocean. That can't happen to me, I thought. I've never even had a simple boat ride. Besides, going to Australia—a country I knew little about and where I didn't know anyone—only increased my anxiety. The chances of making it safely were slim. Even if I did manage to land there, those fears and negative thoughts did nothing to ease the stress that had been building in me recently.

"You haven't done anything yet; nothing has happened. Don't be so scared, and don't jump to the worst conclusions now," I kept telling myself. Despite the overwhelming fears and the worst-case scenarios playing out in my mind, this option remained a possibility. Every time I thought about it, fear gripped me, but I would reassure myself that I didn't have to go through with it—I was just researching different options. Or did I have to? It was worth looking into this strange option. It wouldn't hurt to find out more. I had to start somewhere, anywhere.

This new idea wouldn't leave my mind for a moment. I must do something; I must start somewhere, anything, anywhere. I asked my friend if it was possible for me to meet her relative. Fortunately, she gave a positive answer and arranged a meeting between us. Seeking advice from a total stranger was out of character for me, but considering such a strange and dangerous option for migration was out of character too.

I knew that leaving home for another country in the most unconventional way meant potential dangers, but I kept repeating to myself, "Calm down, nothing has happened yet. It's just a meeting with a new person and asking a few questions to learn more about all possible options." But deep down, I knew I was lying to myself. Perhaps this was the only option left for me, with as little support and as few choices as possible from any other source. Maybe this was the last path to freedom for me, and it was both the best and the worst option at the same time.

Thousands of thoughts and questions crowded my scared, worried, and helpless mind. I couldn't believe it was me considering such a dangerous way to leave this country. But I knew I was done—with everything here, with everything I'd experienced so far, and with all that had happened in my life since the revolution. I wasn't even 18 when the revolution shattered life for many young people like me. I can't take it anymore. The reality is that it might even be too late—I should have done this much earlier. But every time the thought of migration crossed my mind before, false hope stopped me from thinking about this strange idea. Or maybe it wasn't just false hope but the fear of change—a big change. Now, suddenly, I felt courage rising within me, turning that false hope into a stark reality of what should have happened long ago. Today, I'd rather die than continue living like this, with no rights, no choices, and nothing that even remotely resembles freedom.

Thinking "It's now or never" gave me a sense of courage. It made me feel ready to face all the dangers because the hope of achieving a normal life had taken root in me. I had the right to desire a better life. Even just thinking about leaving behind all those oppressive barriers brought a feeling I hadn't experienced yet but was desperate to attain. It could restore the dignity I had lost, or if I ever had it.

Each time I found the courage to consider this last option, I became more convinced that it was the only choice for me, no matter the cost. But I had to admit, the stress of this unusual and unknown route was killing me. Not only the stress, but the fear I tried to deny and even hide from myself, stayed with me all the time, no matter how hard I tried to distract my mind and focus on the sweet result. It was there, and every time it felt stronger than before.

I was so scared, even though it was just an idea. Nothing had happened yet, not even the first steps had been taken. I knew very well that beyond all the natural dangers we might face in the ocean, what frightened me most was the thought of traveling alone in the most unconventional, unclear, and unknown way, with total strangers. But I had always been alone in the journey of life—this time was no different. The only difference was that the shadow of death was closer now, undeniable and unavoidable, and I was ready to face it.

I had no idea what kind of people would accompany me on this risky journey, which could potentially end in tragedy at the bottom of the ocean. I tried to calm myself down by thinking, "When you sit on an airplane, you don't know the other passengers either." You don't know the pilot either. But what a stupid comparison that was! I knew it was foolish, but I did my best to ignore everything that might bring more fear and cause me to abandon this new plan before I even started. Then there would be nothing left but Plan Zero.

All I could think about day and night was getting away from what I called home—a place that lacked peace and left me with disappointment, stress, and fear of being myself. Although leaving in this way might still carry all those unpleasant feelings, or even worse, at least it would end at some point. But this nightmare of a lifestyle would never end. All my efforts to improve my life seemed to lead to a broken heart and the daily erosion of my last bits of confidence.

It was heartbreaking to leave behind my home and belongings in an instant, too preoccupied to fully process the sadness of leaving my identity behind. But what good is an identity when you can't be yourself? It's probably just some papers and documents that don't reflect the real you—the person who has been hiding behind those documents all your life. It's your documented identity, not your soul or your true existence.

I was too stressed to think about anything other than how I could possibly make this journey as smooth as possible. What a joke—even in such a situation, it brought a bitter smile to my face. As if there could be a smooth way for this.

The only option left seemed to be what I was already in the middle of—a chance to go to Australia in the most challenging but fastest way possible, by boat. I had no idea about the experience of traveling by boat to Australia or anywhere else. I was so desperate to escape this hell that I would welcome any possible means, even if it seemed more like suicide than a journey. My mind felt like a crowded bazaar, and I felt like a lost child left behind by her parents in the dark, unsure of where to start or whom to talk to for guidance on this life-threatening journey. Besides, if I chose this unusual, illegal, and socially unacceptable way to migrate, I shouldn't even talk to anyone about it. But who cares about being wise when the word "freedom" keeps ringing in your head constantly?

    I began searching the internet, but information about this particular way of traveling was very limited. I made it clear to myself that no matter what happens, I will not change my mind. I kept repeating it day and night so that I would believe it with every bone and cell in my body. I will not give up until I reach my final goal, even if it means starting from scratch in the face of extreme hardships. Disappearing in the ocean seemed preferable to a life where I had no control over what happens to me or what my next plan might be. The sense of dignity and pride within me was already dead, but perhaps I could revive the last remnants within myself.

    I needed to feel that sense again so much that giving my life for it seemed like nothing at the moment. After all, we all have to pay a price to achieve our dreams. This time, the price for gaining my dreams is my life, and I strongly believe it's worth it. I'm coming to the belief that continuing this life is useless if I can't express the real me. I'm trying hard to pull myself out of that deep well of a comfort zone I've been trapped in all my life by my fears. I don't know how I managed all these years to just follow the same pattern of an unreal life, but something has happened inside me—a spark of sudden change—and I like it so much. I've liked it all my life, but now I can deeply and clearly feel it.

Finally, I met with my never-before-seen travel companion. We spoke on the phone to arrange this meeting, and he was smart enough not to discuss the details over the phone. I invited him to my house for the meeting so my husband could meet him too. Although he was a total stranger to us, for such a conversation, maybe home was the safest and best option rather than a public place like a café.

Because of my husband's quiet demeanor, I knew I had to be careful. One wrong move, one hint of suspicion, and everything I had meticulously planned could fall apart. His calmness was unnerving, like the silence before a storm. Yet, I needed that calmness to persist—at least until I was safely out of the country. Meherdad's youth and confidence presented their own risks, but also a strange comfort. He could easily have been my son, and perhaps that's why my husband wanted to meet him. He needed to ensure I wasn't making a reckless decision, even if it meant trusting another man to accompany me on this perilous journey.

One afternoon, in the middle of spring, the doorbell rang. My heart pounded as I opened the door, with my hands trembling. There he was—Meherdad. Tall, fit, and strikingly handsome, he climbed the stairs toward me. His presence filled the space with an energy that was both calming and unsettling. In his late twenties, Meherdad had the athletic build of a fitness coach, which I later learned he was. He exuded confidence, a stark contrast to the storm of fear that raged within me. Unlike me, he seemed entirely unbothered by the dangers of this journey, perhaps because his younger brother had already made it safely to Australia by boat a few months earlier.

As we talked, I discovered that Meherdad and his brother were close friends with one of my son's old schoolmates—a young man I had known well and had often welcomed into my home when he and my son were nearly inseparable. The fact that someone I knew and trusted had successfully completed the same journey with Meherdad's brother brought me a small measure of relief. It felt like a tiny sign of hope, something to cling to in the midst of overwhelming fear. I remembered how that young man had come to say goodbye before he left the country, though he had said nothing about how he was planning to leave. At the time, I hadn't even known he was heading to Australia. In hindsight, it made sense; I wouldn't have felt safe sharing my plans with others either.

I bombarded Meherdad with questions, trying to extract every detail he might know from his brother's experience. His calm, easy answers only amplified my anxiety. How could he be so relaxed about something so dangerous? Was it his age, or was he simply careless? It was hard for me to grasp. His demeanor, which should have been reassuring, only made me more nervous. Part of me suspected that much of what he said was exaggerated, a mask of confidence to cover the reality of the situation. We were, after all, planning to cross an ocean in a fishing boat—not exactly a luxury cruise. But in my desperation, I wanted to believe him, even if I knew deep down that I was lying to myself.

I was old enough to distinguish between reality and dreams, but in that moment, dreams felt safer. I needed them, because reality was suffocating, no different from the ocean that threatened to swallow me whole. I had to push forward, driven by a strange blend of determination and fear. It was time to act on my decision, even though everything in me screamed to stop and reconsider.

Recognizing the need for caution, I suggested to Meherdad that if he talked about our journey to anyone, he should tell them I was his aunt. This lie would give us a better chance of navigating through any suspicious eyes. He agreed, adding that he hadn't mentioned the true nature of our plans to anyone except his immediate family and girlfriend. From that moment on, I became his "aunt," and surprisingly, the role felt natural. It was as if we both needed to believe in this fabricated relationship to keep our hearts steady. Even years later, when I think of him, he still feels like my real nephew.

Every piece of information about this form of travel felt like a lifeline, but the reality was that there wasn't much to go on. People who knew anything were hesitant to share, and I couldn't exactly explain why I was gathering such sensitive information without raising suspicions. Ever since the revolution and the rise of the current religious regime, trust among people had withered. Spies seemed to be everywhere, hidden among ordinary citizens. Sharing your thoughts and plans could lead to disaster—imprisonment, torture, or worse. This climate of fear made even the simplest tasks fraught with anxiety.

Some of the information we managed to gather felt unreliable, but in our desperation, we clung to whatever we could get. I found myself pretending to ask questions for a neighbor or an acquaintance, just to avoid arousing suspicion. It was a delicate dance of trying to glean useful details while keeping my true intentions hidden.

As I sifted through the scarce information available, I learned that the security police at the airport were increasingly suspicious of passengers traveling to Indonesia, believing many were attempting to reach Australia. This news only added to my anxiety. I told Meherdad that we should first land in Malaysia, a more typical tourist destination for Iranians, and then purchase our tickets to Indonesia from Kuala Lumpur. This detour would, I hoped, help us avoid the intense scrutiny at Tehran's airport. He agreed—everyone knew how easily airport security could cancel your trip without any real reason. They could simply ban you from traveling for any period of time they want at airport. If they did, there would be nothing we could do, and all our plans would be ruined.

Meherdad said that he had a friend working at a travel agency who could arrange the tickets for us. Although I found it difficult to fully trust him, I was relieved that he was handling this part. It allowed me to focus on other tasks, like preparing for the journey and selling off possessions, without raising any red flags among friends and family. The challenge was selling items I used daily without drawing attention to my plans, but I needed the money to fund my escape.

My husband's silence during this time was unusual, adding to my worries. He had always been vocal, constantly nagging about one thing or another. But now, with the letter of attorney in his hands, he seemed indifferent. This strange calmness was both unsettling and a relief. I also did not ask for money from my husband. I knew he had the legal power to stop me from leaving the country at any moment, but I didn't want to give him any reason to exercise that power. So, I softened my tone and tried to maintain peace, knowing these might be our last days together—whether I survived the journey or not.

We had spent many years together, and I didn't want to tarnish our final moments. Deep down, I knew that if I left him for an extended period, he wouldn't remain loyal. But I was the one leaving, and I had learned to endure in silence. There was a part of me that felt guilty for pursuing my dreams and leaving him behind. But I also knew that this was my only chance at freedom.

After a few hours of conversation in the first meeting with Meherdad we agreed to keep in touch only by phone, avoiding in-person meetings to reduce the risk of drawing attention. We decided on coded language for our phone conversations, fully aware that every word could be monitored. Meherdad's youth made him somewhat careless, but his confidence also made him bold. I couldn't afford to be as relaxed as he was; one of us had to be cautious, and that role fell to me—the "aunt."

Despite the risks, there was something I appreciated about Meherdad. From our first meeting, he started calling me "auntie," and although it was part of our cover, it felt genuine. His confidence in our unusual journey grew, but we both knew that a single misstep, especially during our phone conversations, could destroy our plan before it even began. Our next meeting would be at the airport, where we would have to fully embrace our roles as relatives.

Time was running out, and the reality of what was about to happen began to settle in. It was time to sort through everything and prepare for the journey, but I didn't know where to start. How do you decide what to keep and what to leave behind after spending years building a life? In less than a week, I was letting go of everything I had ever known. The sudden detachment I felt was both unsettling and necessary. Perhaps the promise of freedom was so much more valuable that it made this strange feeling bearable. Freedom—what could be more valuable than that?

The negotiations, planning, selling, and buying—the emotional toll of leaving loved ones behind, knowing I might never see them again—were all part of the process of migration. But this journey was different, far more terrifying. When you migrate through the usual path, it's hard, but there's hope for a better life or at least a new experience. If things don't work out, you can always return. But not in my case. This was a matter of life or death. The possibility of not surviving the ocean loomed large in my mind, making everything I did feel like writing my own suicide note. There was no return.

The more I thought about it, the more surreal it became. I was leaving behind everything familiar—my home, my possessions, and my loved ones. The memories associated with each item I touched were overwhelming, especially those tied to my children, my late son, and the life I had built over the years. But I had to remind myself to focus on the bigger picture: the freedom that awaited me, the tomorrow that could be different, *better*.

Yet, no matter how hard I tried to stay positive, fear was a constant companion. This was the most dangerous, most improper way to migrate. Even if I survived the ocean, I would have to face the judgment and blame of those who found out what I had done. But I had to be ready for the drama, for the challenges that lay ahead. Along with the fear, I tried to convince myself that I deserved freedom, that I was entitled to a better life. I wasn't a tree, rooted to one spot—I could move to find happiness, even if it was just a chance.

As I breathed in the air around me, I could feel that it was different from yesterday. It carried the scent of freedom, of something lost that was slowly finding its way back to me. Freedom was real, and maybe it was waiting for me somewhere else in the world. Handing over the letter of attorney to my husband wasn't hard. Saying goodbye, however, was another story. Only a few people knew I was leaving, and even fewer knew the truth about how I planned to do it. I couldn't risk telling many people that I was leaving the country forever.

Living in a country where trust was a rare commodity made everything more complicated. You couldn't confide in anyone, not even those closest to you. Too many people had been betrayed by those they trusted the most. That's why, even when saying goodbye to those few people, I didn't explain how or why I was leaving. There were always nosy relatives who wanted to pry into every detail of your life, but this time, my anxiety helped me stand firm. There was no room for private detectives in my life anymore.

As I prepared for the journey, I found myself surprisingly empowered by the strange energy that came with such a dangerous plan. I thought to myself, "You didn't have to migrate to learn how to deal with nosy family members. You could have done this a long time ago." But perhaps this journey, as risky as it was, had given me the strength I needed to finally take control of my life.

Meherdad managed to get in touch with a few people smugglers in Indonesia, through contacts provided by his friends. Among them, we prioritized the one who had helped his brother. This person seemed more trustworthy, but we couldn't be sure. I had heard too many stories of smugglers who vanished after taking your money, leaving you stranded with no way forward. We decided it was too risky to contact any of them while we were still in Iran, knowing that phone conversations were closely monitored. Even a single mention of a "people smuggler" could trigger the authorities to start listening to all our calls.

We finally agreed that our first contact with the smuggler would be made only after we arrived in Indonesia. From the outside, we might have seemed overly cautious, but after living nearly 40 years under a regime that instilled fear in every aspect of life, I had learned to be scared of everything—even my own shadow, even my closest family members.

Indonesia was not our first destination. As planned, we would first fly to Malaysia, where we would have some time to figure out our next steps. Each step was exhausting, consuming all my energy. But I knew I couldn't afford to waste any of it—every ounce of strength would be needed for what lay ahead. Passing through Iran's airport security gate would be our first major hurdle. Even in the last moments, the security police could find an excuse to stop us, and if they did, there would be no turning back.

At that moment, my only dream was to arrive safely in Indonesia. But even that wouldn't guarantee the success of the rest of our plan. I had heard terrible stories about the corruption among Indonesian police, how they would extort money from Iranian travelers, knowing exactly why we were there. If you didn't bribe them enough, you could end up in one of Indonesia's notorious jails, places so horrific that even thinking about them filled me with fear.

A few months before these plans had taken root in my mind, I had applied for a job at the Indonesian embassy. They had responded positively, inviting me for an interview that never happened. But I thought this might be a good excuse if I needed to confront the Indonesian police upon arrival. It was a slim hope, but it was something to cling to, like a small light in the darkness.

But it was too soon to think about Indonesia and its challenges. First, we had to leave Iran and get through the airport security. One step at a time, I reminded myself. Like Scarlett O'Hara in Gone with the Wind, I told myself, "I'll think about that tomorrow." My mind was full of fears, and every cell in my body was tired. But like a prisoner planning a great escape, I kept pushing myself to be patient, to stay calm.

I desperately wanted to share my thoughts with someone, to relieve some of the overwhelming stress. But the truth was, I realized just how alone I was. There was no one in my life I could confide in. And perhaps that was for the best—the fewer people who knew about my plan, the safer I would be.

Later, I discovered that for Meherdad, traveling with me was also a relief. He felt safer having someone with him, especially since I could speak English, which might come in handy during difficult moments. I also felt reassured by his presence. Despite knowing it was probably false hope, there was some comfort in his strength, his imposing physical presence. If we faced any unexpected dangers, I believed he might be able to protect us, though I knew that expecting such support from anyone was naive.

He comes from a generation that primarily focuses on survival, often thinking only of how to make it possible for themselves. The old-fashioned notions of chivalry and selflessness are rare in this generation. While I don't believe every young person today thinks this way, my experience with those I encountered on this journey reinforced this impression. Most seem to prioritize their own well-being above all else.

In this journey, Meherdad and I had become a strange, makeshift family—an aunt and her nephew, bound together not by blood but by the mutual fear of an uncertain future. This bond, forged in desperation, helped us both push through the stress and anxiety that threatened to overwhelm us. Even though Meherdad pretended not to be affected by it, I knew better. We both needed each other, and this connection, born out of necessity, gave us the strength to carry on.

It's strange how, even after all these years, I still think of him as my nephew. I'm almost certain that if we ran into each other on the street, he wouldn't even recognize me or stop to say hello. He was young then, full of energy and hope for the future, while I was weighed down by the trauma of a life lived under oppression. His youthful optimism contrasted sharply with my weary skepticism.

I let Meherdad handle the ticket purchases. Although he was a stranger, I had to start trusting him at some point. We were about to embark on a much bigger journey together, and so I handed him the money to buy our tickets to Malaysia. We both knew we should buy round-trip tickets to make it seem like we were planning to return to Iran, a necessary deception to avoid suspicion.

I told Meherdad we should practice our story, to make sure we could handle any unexpected questions from nosy people. We talked about our families, our backgrounds, making sure our stories matched. Although we would have plenty of time to practice during the trip, it was better to be prepared in advance, just in case we were questioned at the airport.

We exchanged stories about our families, rehearsing the details so we could convincingly pose as relatives if anyone questioned us. But my stress was so overwhelming that even remembering these simple details was difficult. My brain, overloaded with anxiety, felt like it had lost its capacity to memorize anything. I hated feeling so clumsy, but I had to keep going.

The last days and weeks were a whirlwind of activity, which was a blessing because it left me little time to dwell on my fears. But at night, when everything was quiet, the stress would catch up to me, making it impossible to sleep. I started taking sleeping pills every night, not just to sleep but to escape the relentless anxiety, if only for a few hours. I even considered bringing the pills on the boat to calm my nerves, but then I realized that in an emergency, I would need to be alert. But what good would being alert do if disaster struck? Once I was on the ocean, everything would be out of my hands.

The night before I left the country, I called my son, who was in the Netherlands. I didn't tell him anything about my plans because I was too afraid to bring it up over the phone. Instead, we had our usual chat about mundane things—what I had cooked for dinner, how he had spent his day. As he talked, I quietly cried, knowing this might be the last time I heard his voice. The last time I had seen him was in 2011, during a business trip to the Netherlands. Whether we would reunite in this life or the next, I didn't know, but I held on to the dream of living together in peace someday.

I told him I might be going on a work mission for a while and that I might not be able to contact him for a few weeks. This wasn't unusual, given my job as a business interpreter, so he didn't suspect anything. I was careful not to reveal any details, pretending I had a cold to explain why my voice sounded different—cracked from the tears I was holding back. When I hung up the phone, I was relieved that he hadn't picked up on my lies. It was better this way; I didn't want him to worry.

Finally, the big day came. A day that part of me had been waiting for my whole life, and another part of me desperately wished to postpone. The part of me that wanted to move forward won, but not necessarily because it was stronger—just because it was more determined.

We met again at the airport. I met Meherdad's family for the first time, though I never got to meet my supposed "sister," his mother, who was recovering from surgery. His younger sister, girlfriend, and father accompanied him, while I was there with my husband. The tears I had been holding back threatened to spill over, but I reminded myself to stay composed. I also reminded Meherdad's sister and girlfriend to act naturally, as if we were just heading off on a two-week holiday.

Looking back now, I think if the security police had been smart, they could have easily seen through our charade. Who goes on a holiday to Malaysia with his aunt, especially a young man like Meherdad? Perhaps, the authorities knew who the real holidaymakers were and who wasn't, but they chose to turn a blind eye. Maybe they were glad to get rid of those of us who were unhappy with the system, those who had the potential to rise up in rebellion—something like what we saw in the recent uprisings in Iran, which I'm proud to say were led by young women, a historical first since the revolution.

Chapter Four

We said our final goodbyes, holding each other tight, not knowing if there would ever be a second chance to embrace. Then, we walked toward the gate—the first monster of this game, one of the hardest steps. We had tickets for Malaysia, but despite all my previous business trips and the positive thoughts I tried desperately to inject into my head, I was still stressed. You never know when or why the airport security police might stop and ban you from continuing your travel. Often, you don't even know why they've picked on you; they usually don't need a reason for what they do to people.

It's not uncommon for them to stop people under the pretext of further security checks, only to release them after their flight has already departed. After waiting for hours in their security station, they finally tell the poor passengers they can go—when it's too late. There's never an apology, nor any logical explanation given. They're there to exert their authority, whether legitimate or not. In such cases, you simply have to leave. Questioning them or demanding a reason will only lead to a bigger drama, and if you're lucky, you might escape further unlawful interrogation.

Security was even more rigorous for passengers traveling to Indonesia. Many people who had gone there never returned. The airport security would scrutinize and question anyone with Indonesia as their destination. For us, this part was safer since we planned to transit through another country before reaching Indonesia. The trick of having a round-trip ticket worked well—it reduced suspicion from the security police as they meticulously checked these details at the gates.

We were very careful during those final moments with our family, which likely helped us stay safe during this stage. Even saying goodbye to your loved ones was under their watchful eyes. Why should you show great sadness and shed tears when leaving if it's only a two-week trip? I kept reminding everyone to act normal, though I knew it was difficult, even for myself. It was uncomfortable giving instructions to total strangers on how they should act, but it was necessary.

Passing through each gate was extremely stressful. Every minute, I feared the security police would stop us and aim their intimidating stares at my chest. I tightened my scarf to avoid any issues with my hijab that could cause them to stop me. I had departed from this airport many times in my life, but this time, the fear and horror were far greater than ever before. Even during my work or vacation trips, I had never been completely at ease, but compared to today, those days felt like a walk in the park. On a day to bid farewell without knowing when the next hello might be, even the best actors would struggle to handle it normally.

We tried to walk steadily and quickly, reaching the last gate. My feet were shaking with every step; it felt like heavy stones were tied to them. I could barely push the trolley—it was the heaviest thing in the world for me, and I had no energy left to walk any further. Fortunately, we didn't have much luggage on this journey, but carrying my heavy, frightened body was enough to drain any remaining energy. I took my final steps and settled into the nearest chair in front of the boarding gate.

I breathed deeply, finding a fleeting sense of relief in the dwindling oxygen around me. Meherdad wasn't any better; his face was pale, consumed by the fear of being stopped by the security police in those last moments. The confidence he had shown earlier was nowhere to be seen. I offered him a piece of chocolate from my bag, and we both silently sat in our seats, fully aware of the implications of leaving the country this way and the potential dangers that awaited us. To alleviate the stress, I began texting my childhood friend, leaving her my final words and instructions on what to do if I were to perish in the ocean. She was among the very few who knew I was leaving for good, though she didn't know the exact route I had chosen. In this text, which might be my last words, she would finally know—words I couldn't bring myself to say in person.

After handing over our luggage, receiving our boarding cards, and passing through the security gate, the look the man at the security gate gave us seemed like he was trying to catch the most notorious criminal trying to escape. This was not an unfamiliar look; they always give you that look. Their policy is to instill fear in people to maintain control. Thankfully, this part passed safely, and now it was time to walk to our flight gate. Finally, a young woman in a blue uniform opened the gate, checking our tickets and boarding passes. Although she had a beautiful face, she was in full hijab, and I told myself I hoped never to see such a uniform or outfit again in my life.

We sat at our gate, not for long, but long enough to feel every heartbeat. Through all these steps, we exchanged no words, which must have seemed strange for two people supposedly on a happy vacation, but I guess we simply couldn't talk. All our energy was focused on acting as normal as possible.

We walked in silence toward the airplane. Both of us were shaking and counting our steps to our respective seats. The stewardess guided us to our seats, though I could barely hear anything over the pounding of my heart. Our seats were a bit apart from each other, which was fine. Perhaps it was for the best; we probably needed some distance and privacy from each other since neither of us wanted to discuss the circumstances at hand.

I could barely hear the stewardess's standard safety instructions and flight details, but I kept my gaze fixed on her actions and gestures. I wasn't ready to engage in conversation with the man seated next to me, even though he seemed very happy and eager to talk. His excitement assured me he was really going to Malaysia for a holiday, not like us. I think it was his first time traveling abroad, as he seemed very happy and excited. His excited voice about how the flight might be convinced me that I definitely could not be good company for him during this flight. The best thing to do was to pretend I had a headache, close my eyes, and try to block out my thoughts, even though it was impossible to shut down my mind.

As the plane took off, its sound tore my heart between the sorrow of leaving my home forever and the happiness that this journey had finally begun. I stole my final glances at home through the plane window and took a deep breath. It was over—not completely, but everything I had known in this country was over. My feelings for my home would always remain the same, as would my hatred for those who occupied my home and forced thousands of us to leave in all different ways.

Whether I died or survived, this chapter of my life, which had mostly been filled with unpleasant memories, was over. But I still couldn't take my eyes off the view—my last glance at what I had always called home, a place where I was treated like a total stranger. I was leaving and running away from the rulers of this home, but not from my home itself and my people, whom I would always love. These two are completely different subjects. Authorities and rulers who continually govern with dictatorship policies are like irresponsible parents—you want to run away from them, but you still feel love for the true meaning of parenthood. It's a close relationship between love and hate.

I repeated in my thoughts: whether I survived this ordeal or not, these would be my last views of the place I had called home my entire life, at least for a while. This home was not safe or comforting, never gave me a sense of being loved and respected, but it was home—a home I might never see again. Now, what can I call myself? Perhaps from now on, I'll be considered to be homeless.

My homeland, a place that had never been kind to me, nor to any other woman who lived there, for that matter. A place of endless restrictions, threats, and red flags—for me and countless other women like me, and I must say, men didn't have it much better either. Their laws and regulations only favored those in power and those connected to them. There might seem to be rules in the constitution in favor of the country's citizens, but they are simply words without actions when it comes to benefiting the authorities.

I, like the majority of the country's population, remained a second-class citizen, subject to double standards. To succeed and achieve based on merit, one must either be part of the corrupt establishment or give up entirely. I didn't want to be either—part of the establishment or someone who gives up. At the same time, I had to give the meaning of "home" back to those who had stolen the comfort and safety from us.

The flight wasn't particularly long, as I was accustomed to lengthier journeys, but it provided enough time to push back my stress and find moments of calm. The man sitting next to me soon realized I wasn't going to be good company during the trip, so after noticing my closed eyes, he quietly moved on and began mingling with other passengers, asking for tips on the best places for fun and shopping.

Meherdad, however, appeared to have completely forgotten the reason we were here and all the stress we had experienced at the airport. He was happily chatting with fellow passengers and teasing the beautiful stewardesses. I thought, let him be happy for now, as more difficult times and stresses awaited him. God only knows how much I needed this family member who had unexpectedly entered my life. It felt as though sharing the burden of fear with someone made it easier to bear, although it wasn't guilt I felt, but fear. Perhaps it was selfish of me to find solace in his presence during such a dangerous journey, but I knew he was also expecting a promising future in another country. The hope for a better life for young people was becoming increasingly scarce in our homeland.

A few hours later, the pilot's voice announced that we had reached Malaysia airport and would soon be landing. It was midnight. Despite my exhaustion, I couldn't manage to sleep for even a few minutes during the flight. However, I noticed Meherdad had fallen asleep a few times whenever I checked on him. Though I was extremely tired, sleep eluded me. I desperately needed a place to relax and recharge.

I was longing to lie down in a hotel bed, but we had agreed not to spend too much money in Malaysia. Everything in Kuala Lumpur airport was going smoothly, and it was a fun and nice place. We needed to find the fastest flight to Indonesia, but first, we had to wait until the next day to buy tickets. We later found out there were no flights scheduled for the next two days. This wasn't a typical trip like the ones I had taken before. We had no idea how much the people smugglers might charge us. There was no standard fee for such transactions. If we couldn't convince them to accept the money we had, and they demanded more, we would have to turn back. Neither Meherdad nor I wanted that.

Therefore, we had to be cautious with every cent we spent before dealing with the smugglers. We decided to spend those two days in the airport instead of going to a hotel. We were exhausted from the flight and hungry. In the food court, we grabbed a bite to eat and took turns napping. One of us had to keep an eye on our luggage while the other slept.

I told Meherdad to sleep first. He rested his head on the food court table and fell asleep immediately. I, too, desperately needed sleep, but I tried to distract my mind by observing the people who came to the food court. However, within seconds, the thoughts of what lay ahead and the fear of what might happen consumed me again. I made a concerted effort to divert my tired mind, but this forced distraction had to happen repeatedly. What if…? What if not…? I couldn't blame it all on the way we were traveling; part of it came from the cautious attitude you learn through life. As you get older, this cautiousness hits you harder, especially in difficult situations.

The worst-case scenario of drowning in the ocean played out in my mind, though there could be even worse outcomes. But I wasn't ready to die. I needed another distraction to keep from getting lost in my worries over and over again.

Living in the airport without proper rest wasn't easy, even if it was only for two days. During those moments, I found myself thinking that we could be here like others, just having a good time and fun. These thoughts especially grew stronger when I saw happy passengers running from one gate to another, amazed by the shopping. Although it was very hard and physically draining, those two days of transit finally passed. We almost stayed in one spot—the food court—except for one day when Meherdad insisted on going out of the airport to at least visit the famous Twin Towers in Malaysia.

For him, visiting airport shops and the attractions didn't seem too bad, as it was his first time traveling overseas. But for me, it was neither new nor interesting, especially with all the difficulties I had to endure. Perhaps for him, the excitement came from his age. Maybe I was too old to enjoy it. At the same time, I couldn't shake the worry about my age, which kept reminding me I was too old for traveling like this. But is there an age limit for seeking freedom? Definitely not. I know there's a lot more in daily life that neither surprises you anymore nor attracts you, but what is always attractive and interesting at any age is the freedom to be yourself. That was what we wished to get our hands on soon.

No matter if we were from different generations, the taste of freedom was the most important thing for both of us, and for everyone else we would meet later in this journey. Maybe it was fate that my travel mate would be from a generation far removed from mine, to make me realize that at the end of the day, the most important thing in life is how much freedom and control you can have over your own days and time. This time, we had to create this freedom from the broken pieces of our lives.

I was far too tired from the lack of sleep and proper rest, but I kept telling myself to prepare for the possibility that this might be the easiest part of the trip. I reminded myself that things could get even harder and worse. Be ready; maybe this is just practice for confronting more difficult situations.

Fortunately, we had access to free computers in a section of the airport. Just to kill time, I went to an internet café to check my email and Facebook, hoping to enjoy this forced pleasure for a moment. I was so surprised when I checked my Facebook page and found lots of birthday messages from friends—oh, it was my birthday! I had completely forgotten, too preoccupied with all the stressful subjects surrounding me to remember. Checking and answering the birthday messages, I suddenly realized that this might be my last birthday. With a bitter smile on my face, I thought, maybe this is it—no more birthday wishes on Facebook in the future. But then, I wouldn't be around to answer them, so let's celebrate it with my nephew.

I bought coffee and cake for Meherdad and myself, pretending to celebrate my birthday, but in reality, I wanted to kill the dark and bitter thoughts attacking my tired head all the time with the sweetness of the cake. There was a big smile on my face, but I wasn't happy at all—who could be happy in such circumstances? Meherdad seemed happy, and that confident look returned to his face, but I knew he wasn't truly happy either. The doubt about whether I had made the right decision never left me for a minute. But I also knew it was now or never. Once you hit the road, curiosity about what comes next won't let you stop, and sometimes that curiosity keeps you going. Whatever it was, I had to welcome it.

The hardest and most awful part of those two days was sleeping on the very uncomfortable benches in the airport. Honestly, it was like torture. But anytime my mind was dragged to the probable situations waiting for me in the ocean, it seemed not as bad after all. I felt like an athlete practicing to get their body ready for a bigger competition.

In fact, compared to what I anticipated for the next leg of this journey, the uncomfortable situation in the airport seemed like nothing. Anyway, after two very tiring and uncomfortable days in the airport, we purchased tickets for Jakarta. While we were wandering around the airport, Meherdad called a few smugglers whose numbers were given to him. We no longer had to worry about our phones being monitored; we both had our cell phones with us, but even if our numbers were being tracked, there was nothing anyone could do now. He discussed their prices and other details, such as their plans for setting sail and, most importantly, the condition of the boat they would be using, how many days we would be on the boat, and any other questions that came to mind. We had heard before that these boats were usually old, damaged, and unreliable, posing even greater danger.

The reason was that none of these boats were supposed to return to the starting point. Once the boat reached its destination, if it reached its destination, they would sink it. Most of them were so old that they could hardly make the journey safely. That's why the oldest and most problematic boats, considering their technical conditions, were chosen by smugglers. It was clear they didn't want to risk their financial turnover, and the financial turnover was obviously more important to them than people's lives. After all, they believed that if you were so determined to risk your life, why should they care whether you survive or not?

Although there was no guarantee that their answers to our questions would be truthful, they all knew well how to wrap the ugly reality of less chance for survival in beautiful and shiny promises, guaranteeing no need to worry, that everything would be good, that nothing bad would happen, and that the boats were in great condition. Among them, we selected one smuggler who was more recommended and who had given us his contact details before. Also, Meherdad's brother, who had gone through the same process, had told Meherdad that he had heard good comments from people he met in the detention center that this particular smuggler was more caring about his passengers.

For us, the term "more caring" translated to fewer lies. Meherdad said this particular smuggler had successfully facilitated similar journeys for people he knew in his neighborhood. He gave Meherdad some advice during their first phone conversation, such as instructing him to buy a SIM card as soon as we arrived in Jakarta and to call him. Then he would lead us to the next required steps. He also mentioned whom we should contact straight away; the guy must be one of his staff working in this field. Oh, getting to Jakarta—when would it happen? When would this total nightmare be over? But arriving in Jakarta was not the end of the nightmare; it was just another beginning.

    The time came to board the plane for Jakarta, but at the boarding gate, the staff seemed to single out passengers with Iranian passports for questioning. There are too many passengers for Jakarta every day, and the airport staff knew perfectly well what the reason was and the difference between passengers—whether they were real visitors or after something more important. They probably thought that if you were after a fun journey, you would already be in Malaysia, enjoying yourself there. Why would you go to Indonesia unless there was another reason? And, in fact, for almost all Iranians flying from Malaysia to Indonesia, this was true. With their not-so-friendly gestures, they bombarded us with harsh questions—why we were going to Indonesia, where we intended to stay, how long we planned to stay. Endless questions made me think there was not much difference between them and the security police gates in Iran, which I had stupidly thought would be less of an obstacle here. They emptied all our luggage and searched every item separately. I was so embarrassed, my personal belongings laid out for all these men to scrutinize, and the same was done to Meherdad's luggage. Meherdad also stared at all my scattered belongings, and I was more anxious about him seeing my personal items than the security guards. I was sure I would never see these guards again, but it was hard for me to look at Meherdad when my private things were spread out in front of him. One thing was certain: this was not the end of such humiliations required for this style of travel, but just the beginning.

I tried my best to convince them that we were simply tourists traveling to Indonesia after having a good time in Malaysia, even though I knew they didn't believe us. But unlike others, my English was fluent, which was a great bonus at the time. Also, the email I mentioned earlier, the one I had from the Indonesian Embassy in Tehran, helped a lot. It made them believe us and let us pass the gate easier than others. When I was passing the gate, I saw a long queue of Iranians still being questioned. With even a short glance, you could easily sense the fear and stress in their flushed faces, which convinced me they were all here for the same reason.

To be honest, seeing people from my country in the same situation was a bit of a comfort—I wasn't alone. In this case, the more people in the same boat, the more selfish comfort you feel. At the same time, it deeply broke my heart. Our people, just a few decades ago, used to travel abroad just to spend weekends and school holidays, and that was normal for most people as the level of welfare was stable in the community. Now, such humiliations among my people were not just for the hope of a better life, but for pursuing basic human rights. It was all so sad, but there was no choice other than acceptance.

The large number of people in the same situation as we were, and the fact that they were being forced to stay in the airport because they couldn't give any logical answers to the security police, made the guards almost believe we were traveling to Indonesia for fun. I think Meherdad's good appearance, with luxury and expensive outfits, helped to convince them too. And for myself, acting perfectly like a businesswoman was effective in convincing them we were different. We used the same trick in Jakarta when we faced the corrupt security police there. Otherwise, they could easily have checked our arrival date in Kuala Lumpur and doubted our story of seeking more fun. Thank God they were either too busy to check or too careless—whatever the reason, it worked in our favor.

Although they emptied all our luggage and checked every little thing we had in our suitcases, hoping to find more evidence to prove we weren't real tourists, they couldn't find anything. They seemed a bit angry, and one of them, with a harsh voice, asked me why I was traveling so lightly.

I answered with a big fake smile on my face, "Because we are Iranian, and we love to shop. I promise, we won't come back with light luggage like this. If you're lucky enough to see me on our way back, you'll understand." He didn't respond with words but gave me a sneaky smile, as if to say, "You can't fool me." But luckily, I did. What gave me the feeling of victory was that, whether I could fool him and his colleagues in Kuala Lumpur airport or not, he didn't have any more evidence to prove my real intention for traveling to Indonesia, and that made us the winners of this not-so-pleasant game.

Eventually, they allowed us to proceed and board the plane. I really wished all others could pass this step easily too. In fact, I must say, they didn't make it too difficult for us compared to others. Or maybe because I was constantly preparing myself for the worst-case scenario, it didn't hit me as hard as I expected. But still, the extensive questioning was overwhelming. In reality, the security police's job was to add more stress when we didn't need it at all, given that enough fear and stress awaited us in the near future.

Finally, we boarded the plane. Leaning my head against the seat, we had gotten almost the cheapest flight, so no service at all, but we didn't care. Just sitting on the plane after all those harsh moments was enough for us. Meherdad seemed to feel the same because as soon as we sat down, he fell asleep, but for me, sleep was impossible. I suddenly remembered I hadn't called my husband from the airport to inform him about what we had been through and that we were on our way to Indonesia. Something inside me was telling me I hadn't missed the opportunity—he didn't care that much anyway, and that's why I forgot, whether intentionally or subconsciously.

This journey also gave me a chance to review all the things I didn't want to believe all these years. Maybe from this point on, I should stop all the mistaken paths I had been following, paths I was aware of but didn't have the courage to change. Whether it was a result of being afraid of change or its consequences, I knew very well what and where the source of wrongs in my life was. Sometimes it was the way I followed my job obligations, other times it was my personal interactions, and so on. I guess those who are willing to endure the expenses and consequences of this way of migration are not only seeking a positive change in their lifestyle but also a change in whatever mistakes they made with their wrong decisions or attitudes.

It's a total demolition in every way possible to build a completely new structure. Everything starts from scratch again, like being a newborn infant once more. But this time, there are no parents—just you and yourself to look after. On second thought, a bittersweet hope shone in my heart. There was never such support in your life, and here you are now. So, have hope—maybe the future is far brighter than what you think.

Late at night, the plane finally landed at Jakarta airport. It wasn't cold, and I didn't feel cold in my body, but deep down inside, all my cells were frozen with stress. I was careful all the time not to let Meherdad find out my true feelings. I think he was doing the same, as he seemed happy, at least before we had to face the security police in Jakarta airport. I had heard a lot of bad comments about how unfairly they treat passengers, especially those from countries like Iran. Anyway, as soon as we landed, they categorized passengers and separated those with Iranian passports from others.

I could easily feel the stress and fear on each of our faces—it was inevitable. I knew if I acted like the others, we would be done. Meherdad kept saying he wasn't afraid of anything, but his pale face told a different story. We were taken to a chamber filled with four or five guys, all wearing uniforms. From the moment we entered the room, the questioning started—real hard and verbally violent questioning. All of them had big frowns on their faces and a gesture of disbelief that made me think they had already decided not to believe us, no matter what we said or how hard we tried to convince them. It was late at night, and me being so tired made their faces seem even scarier and uglier than they might really be.

For all of us, it was so evident that their main intention was to extort money from us, and they didn't care about anything else. Their corrupt attitude reminded me of that woman who censored my translations. I wasn't just scared, stressed, and worried—also the terrible feeling of being humiliated was killing me at the same time. We had been warned about this beforehand, as they target passengers from Iran and Afghanistan much more than others. I think they don't even dare to do the same for passengers from European countries or similar places.

I must say they somehow succeeded in instilling fear in you and terrifying you with their angry faces and scary attitude. In the second step, when they had scared you enough, the scam plan came into place. I found a lot in common between these security monsters in Iran and here. Their stern faces, dark and shiny skin, and thin mustaches could easily be likened to the security police in Iran. One thing they were good at, because they had enough practice, was creating fear and harsh situations, as this is the key to winning the game, and this is what makes it easier for them to solicit bribes.

It wasn't a sudden, unexpected situation, everyone had warned me about the corruption of the Indonesian police. So I had prepared myself by thinking about different possible scenarios, and I think that's why I could overcome my fears. We both sides of this stupid theater knew the reality—that all these harsh questions were just a means to blackmail people. Every passenger knows very well that they couldn't care less about what is in your mind regarding your final destination.

But as with other parts of this game, this scene had to pass too, and there was no easier way unless you shut their mouths with a large amount of money. If they can extort money from you, they have no further interest and will let you go. The amount of money they demand varies depending on how intimidated you appear.

Question after question, some of which they didn't even wait for you to answer. Meherdad couldn't speak English, and his face was pale with fear, clearly shaking. But he made an excuse that it was because he was hungry and hadn't eaten for some hours. He was too proud to admit he was scared—a common attitude like many other men from the Middle East. Society, culture, and tradition always dictate that men are never scared of anything nor ever cry for anything. I gave him something sweet I had in my bag, like a good auntie. While he was eating it, I told him to compose himself. Maybe such situations strengthened the feeling that he was really my nephew. I was clearly acting like a good mother, always carrying something in their bag for their kids, and this continued throughout the entire journey—not only for him but for many others. I mean, whatever I had, I shared with others.

As they kept their confusing question party going, I showed them the work invitation email I had obtained from the Indonesian Embassy in Iran. Oh my God, what a great refuge that email was! I tried my best to appear calm—I even surprised myself and didn't know what a good actress I could be. I believe that by presenting this letter, they hesitated to continue their blackmail tactics, as they were aware that their actions were against the law. Perhaps they also feared that such a letter could bring trouble upon them if they persisted. At the very least, it was a different response from the typical lies they hear from other passengers almost every day.

Later, when I met others in the same situation as us, I found out we were the only ones among them who weren't blackmailed—or rather, they couldn't blackmail us. Yes, that's a better way to say it, and it gives me a better level of confidence. To tell the truth, although this was also a scary and stressful step in this trip, I kind of enjoyed it because, as I said, my language ability was something they weren't used to among passengers from this part of the world. That made them believe maybe we weren't the ones they were after. I could also easily feel they were uncomfortable questioning me—it was clearly obvious from their gestures, the apparent fear they had that they might get caught this time. Continuing to bother this one was not a wise decision—let her go; there are always others we can make money from. While they exchanged looks with each other, I could read their minds.

Part of their doubt and fear came from the fact that I played my role as a real tourist perfectly. To be honest, one of the reasons I was so good in those harsh moments was for joy. I felt a sense of setting them up with a devilish smile—kind of a revenge for all the blackmail they had done to poor people. After all, it was some fun I needed to continue. Don't blame me; I needed some fun to endure this lousy trip.

My made-up story was that I had come to Indonesia as a tourist because I wanted to learn more about the country and its culture and traditions, which would help me serve better before starting my work at the Indonesian Embassy in Iran. I continued with a very calm expression on my face, saying how excited I was about this new position and how essential it was to learn more about the culture and traditions of the Indonesian people. The longer this game continued, the more I enjoyed it—I didn't want it to stop. I explained that I had asked my nephew to accompany me on this trip because it might be interesting for him as well, as it's always more fun to have a family member with you when traveling. I imagine they probably thought, "Oh, another lie, but a different lie—one that could potentially be true. And if by a one-in-a-million chance it is true, then blackmailing this one could leave us in huge trouble."

The more fear and doubt I saw in their eyes, the more courageous I felt to continue this interesting game. Looking at my calm and curious face, they probably thought it was better not to take any risks. They could always extort money from others. After all, there are always Iranians and Afghans tired of the oppressive regimes in their homelands who choose this path as an escape. There are always frightened individuals for them to prey upon.

It was better for them to avoid risks and let us go, and that's how we managed to evade paying the corrupt Indonesian police. But when they told us we could leave the airport, I was enjoying the game so much that I didn't want to end it so soon. I even came back to the room, "Oh officer, is there any place you can suggest for us to visit first?" Their angry faces, knowing they hadn't managed to extract any money from us, were even more frowned upon—it was just a few minutes before they would explode. They looked at each other with an unbelievable look, feeling sorry they couldn't handle me the way they were used to. Meherdad felt a bit of relief when they let us go and almost yelled at me in Farsi, "Bia Berrrim".[1]

I continued, "Oh, don't bother; it doesn't matter. I'll ask the hotel reception," and said goodbye with a huge smile on my face. Meherdad couldn't understand the details of our conversation, but he was so surprised by my nutty attitude. Since he couldn't speak English, he was just left with fear and missed the best part of this game—setting up these corrupt officers. Later in the hotel, I described every detail of my conversation with the officers. Even now, after all those years, this is the only fun memory I have from that trip. It gives me huge joy when I remember those officers' pitiful looks and the way they were confused about what to do with me.

Later, I heard from my boat mates that during the same process, they were all extorted for varying amounts of money, ranging from $200 to $7,000. That convinced me they deserved the game I played with them. For sure, they needed even more fear, although with all the fear in the world, the cruelty they inflicted on those desperate passengers in such awkward moments wouldn't be enough to compensate for the money they ripped off the most desperate people to fulfill their hunger for corruption and blackmail. They didn't do it to protect their borders—that would definitely be a different story.

I've always been grateful for being able to speak English, but this time, being able to communicate verbally really saved me. They tried various unclear methods to coax money out of me. Although I managed to escape from these

---

1 Let's go!

scammers, the story was different for many others. Those who lost all the money they had with them had to ask for money from their family back home, and those who weren't blessed enough with family support had to turn back with huge disappointment and depression, even before being able to have a few days of fun in Indonesia.

It might seem unbelievable, but these were among the stories we heard from other passengers, and I personally believe them since I witnessed myself that the Indonesian police had no mercy for any of us. Their attitude convinced me the Indonesian police were no better than the security or morality police in Iran. In similar situations, they probably treat poor Indonesian people even worse.

While we were walking to the exit to get a taxi, I took a deep breath and reassured myself that this would be the last formal hurdle before reaching our destination. Later, I found out that whether formal or informal, there was nothing relaxing about this trip—not for me, at least.

Chapter Five

Both of us had clearly the same thing in our mind, but neither of us brought up the subject. It felt like we were trapped in a labyrinth game, something like computer games, encountering one obstacle after another. Winning doesn't require much intelligence, or at least that was what I was thinking. Part of the winning process is luck, and the other part may be attributed to your destiny. The prize, if you win at the end of the game, is your life. So, you must pay close attention to every little move you make. Your first mistake may be your last.

This thought lingered in the back of our minds, anticipating the next episode of horror, the next monstrous obstacle in this labyrinth. We both knew that this was just the beginning, and perhaps one of the easiest parts of the game.

Outside the airport, a very pleasant light spring breeze offered a momentary relief, and I felt it in every cell of my skin. It was like I was drinking this lovely breeze with my skin, and its coolness took me high into the skies. The breeze amazed me while we were waiting for a taxi in the captivating midnight atmosphere. The taxi driver could speak a bit of English, but not very well. It was enough to answer simple questions, like, "Can you take us to a hotel that's not too far from the city and has reasonable prices?" He took us to a hotel near the airport, but before settling on one, we checked a few others. Our first priority was how close it was to the city as a sign of its safety, and of course, the price was another important factor to consider. We had to be cautious with our expenses; we had no idea how long we'd be staying in Jakarta.

I had heard stories of people waiting for months in Jakarta before they could travel by boat. Some even went to the UNHCR to start the asylum process, and waited years without any guarantee their cases would be accepted. No, I didn't have enough money to wait that long. Besides, Meherdad was with me now, but if it took too long, he would definitely leave me. What could a lonely woman do in this country? Although he really was not that much help, he kept my heart warm knowing a family member was with me.

I tried to kill all negative thoughts—oh no, not now, not at the beginning, when nothing had started yet. I kept telling myself this country, even in the first few hours of our arrival, was definitely a safe place for me. It was too late to think otherwise.

My head was about to burst from strange thoughts that wouldn't leave me, not even for a second. Maybe I seemed too cautious to some people, but I knew deep down this was no ordinary journey.

I had to consider every possibility, especially when I was alone in this. Yes, my beloved nephew was with me now, but that was only temporary. Why wouldn't he? Not only because we're not truly related by blood, but because it's an unwritten rule in life to save yourself when things get tough. Not everyone is like that, but this nephew I see now is not one of those action-movie heroes, even though he looks like he could play the part.

Eventually, we settled on a hotel that fit our budget and was close to residential areas. It resembled a third-grade motel with minimal facilities, but it offered disco nights, which thrilled Meherdad. He insisted we take this one, and I agreed, seeing how excited he was when the receptionist mentioned the disco. His happiness left me little choice. After all, the poor quality of the motel didn't bother me much, so why not let him enjoy it?

Meherdad came from a generation shaped by the aftermath of the revolution, burdened with restrictions in life. As a boy, he had only seen real discos in movies. This was his first time traveling abroad, and the freedom he was experiencing made him eager to try everything new. I couldn't blame him. For him, freedom meant exploring and tasting a life he had never known. I was past that phase of life, with different experiences, but freedom has many meanings. For women in my country, just walking with the wind blowing through our hair is a dream of freedom. In contrast, for women elsewhere, such a simple thing might not even seem significant.

A lobby man, who wasn't much help since we carried our own luggage, led us to our room. It was on the fourth floor, and we soon discovered the hotel had no elevator. Tired as we were, we had to haul our luggage up the narrow stairs. I couldn't stop grumbling about how the receptionist hadn't informed us. You could imagine our faces as we struggled up the stairs, though, fortunately, our bags weren't too heavy. Under different circumstances, this scene would have made me laugh.

At last, we arrived at our room. It was small and not very tidy, as I had expected, with just one double bed. I began to yell in frustration about how the receptionist hadn't mentioned there would only be one bed when I'd asked for two. The lobby man, with his limited English, tried to explain it wasn't his fault. There was no phone in the room to call reception, and I was too exhausted to go back downstairs. Meherdad didn't seem to mind, so I decided to let it go. I told him I would sleep on the floor. Although I knew I wouldn't get a good night's rest, my maternal instincts told me to let him have the bed.

The room was humid and far from comfortable, but it was still better than the benches at the airport. As a reward for my small sacrifice, I decided I deserved to take a shower first. The moment we dropped our bags, Meherdad decided to explore the area, even though it was late. I was glad he left. It meant I could shower and get dressed without worrying about the usual modesty we Iranian women feel. The shower was warm, and after the last few days, washing away the grime was a small luxury.

When I finished, Meherdad hadn't returned, so I took my time getting dressed. He came back just as I was going through my luggage, and it was his turn to shower. While he was in the bathroom, I pulled out some canned food and bread I had packed. It was cold and tasteless, but it filled our stomachs, and more importantly, it saved us money. Meherdad ate quickly, not because he was hungry, but because he was eager to join the disco he had seen earlier.

After we ate, I cleaned up, while he got ready in front of the mirror, reminding me of myself at his age—always eager for new experiences, full of energy. But now, sitting in this run-down room with its old, worn furniture, all I could think about was the next step in our journey and the challenges that awaited us.

Before he left for the disco, we briefly discussed the next day's plans. Our first priority was to buy a SIM card so Meherdad could contact the smugglers he had numbers for and compare prices. The very thought of smugglers made me nervous; I didn't even want to speak to them on the phone. But I was too tired to think about it further. I wanted to hold on to the simple joy of being clean and having a mattress, even if it wasn't the best.

While Meherdad headed to the disco, I let the soft pillows draw me into sleep. I had been deprived of the basic comforts of cleanliness and a bed for days. Though the bed wasn't perfect, it was more than enough for me. He could enjoy the disco while I enjoyed some much-needed rest. Sleeping on the floor wasn't ideal, but it was better than what I had endured recently.

These simple comforts—like a bed and a shower—are things we take for granted, much like the sun. We see it every day and forget it's even there. I realized how easy it is to overlook these blessings. It reminded me of my years with my children. They were always with me, but in the hustle of daily life, I sometimes forgot to truly appreciate their presence. It's true what they say—the best things in life are free.

When he left the room, I eagerly jumped onto the makeshift bed—just a blanket and pillows spread on the floor—which was enough to re-energize my tired body. I collapsed easily, letting my exhausted body sink into the cold floor. The clean smell of the blanket helped mask the discomfort of sleeping on the hard surface. I needed to regain my energy for the next day, when we would have to make important decisions, like contacting the people smugglers.

The blanket worked its magic, and I fell into a deep sleep immediately. I didn't even realize what time Meherdad came back. It was nice of him to be quiet when he entered—something that many Iranian men often overlook.

The next morning, I woke up early while Meherdad was still asleep. I knew he had probably stayed up all night, and waking him wouldn't do much good. Besides, we weren't close enough for me to feel comfortable disturbing his rest. I didn't want to upset him or provoke a reaction. So, I waited until he woke up naturally, even though I was anxious about losing another day. Every lost day meant another night in the hotel and more expenses, but I reassured myself that with people smugglers, there isn't a strict time to contact them—they are used to dealing with odd hours. I was impressed by how well Meherdad handled these kinds of situations. In many cases, he seemed more composed than I was.

It was nearly midday when he finally woke up. I tried to stay calm and quiet, though my stress was rising. He seemed well-rested, even though he didn't admit it. When we were both ready, we went downstairs to ask the receptionist where we could buy a SIM card. The receptionist, with a knowing look, directed us to any news agency where we could get one.

It was an unbearably hot day, and I was desperate for coffee or tea, as was Meherdad. We both started sweating while asking for the SIM card from the news agency. I bought two soft drinks and some cake from a nearby food truck, enough to give us a boost of energy. Interestingly, throughout the trip, Meherdad acted as though it was my responsibility to feed him, almost as if I were his real aunt. I didn't mind at first, but since we both had limited money, it felt unusual. There was no reason for me to always pay for him.

At first, it seemed okay to handle a few meals, but I knew that if I kept paying for him, it would become impossible to support both of us, especially since we didn't know how long we'd be stuck in Jakarta. Many people before us had faced long waits, and it was common to stay in Indonesia for months before securing passage. I avoided bringing up money, feeling embarrassed to ask him to contribute, but I was annoyed because it seemed deliberate that he never offered to pay. I convinced myself that maybe spending a bit helped distract me from the stress of the trip. I also wondered if Meherdad might not have enough money and was too embarrassed to say so, but even if that were true, it didn't excuse putting all the financial burden on me.

I knew it was foolish to keep pretending, but I had to push these negative thoughts aside. There were already enough challenges on this journey, and I didn't need to create more. I didn't want to alienate the only relative I had, fake or not. Bringing up money so early in the trip could ruin whatever family connection we had, even if I wasn't happy about it.

Later, I learned that not only did Meherdad have enough money, but he acted the same way with his friends. Some of them even complained about how stingy he was. Everyone is different, and even if he were my real nephew or son, this wasn't the time to confront him about his behavior. I knew that once we hopefully settled in Australia, our lives would separate, and we'd both go our own ways. Observing him throughout the trip made it clear what kind of person he was.

For me, staying silent wasn't just about generosity—it was also about needing someone by my side. Paying for him was a price I had to pay, and we both knew it. What neither of us realized was that he needed my presence just as much as I needed his. Yes, money was important, but now was the time to focus on bigger issues. I kept reminding myself not to waste energy on small problems, like Meherdad not paying his share. It wasn't worth dwelling on. There were far bigger things to worry about, like matters of life and death. I had to think bigger.

We already had several contact numbers for people smugglers. It seemed there were different groups involved in human trafficking, each with their own methods—almost like travel agencies, in a dark sense. They took clients through different routes and offered varying options. The contact details weren't secret; we had received this information before leaving our country. Meherdad had already called one smuggler from the airport in Malaysia, but we still had other options. It was better to call each one separately, but who could guarantee they were telling the truth?

The reality was that none of them could truly be trusted. We had no choice but to call them, ask for their prices, and gather as much information as we could. Trust, in this context, was a foolish idea. What could we expect from smugglers, after all?

Obviously, we couldn't have made these calls from home, as phone lines in Iran were monitored by the security police. Discussing such matters over the phone would have been far too risky. But now, despite my fears, I had to push forward. My mind kept circling back to one phrase: "Let tomorrow handle it." That line from *Gone with the Wind*—constantly repeated by Scarlett O'Hara—kept running through my thoughts. In a way, it was comforting, helping me push away the overwhelming fear of the present moment.

Meherdad put the phone on speaker so we could both listen. We decided the last smuggler we spoke to seemed the best option. Meherdad knew people who had traveled through him, and they had safely made it to Australia. Among them was his own younger brother and my son's childhood friend, which reassured me. The price this smuggler offered was also more reasonable compared to the others.

I was trying to discern something about his personality from his voice, which, in hindsight, was foolish. How could I possibly understand someone's character just by hearing their voice? But I guess a lot of unreasonable thoughts fill your mind when you're feeling insecure—so desperate that you try to cling to anything that might bring you even the slightest sense of survival. Meherdad was much calmer compared to me, as usual, and that calmness definitely came from the hope young people often have, regardless of circumstances.

Based on my sensory impression, what I could hear in his voice was a strong, stern tone—a voice belonging to a man whose character and intentions remained unknown to me. He arranged for us to meet in an undisclosed location, emphasizing that a crowded public place like a café wouldn't be safe for him, though I personally would have preferred it.

I had limited information about this man; all I knew came from what I had heard during our conversations and the fact that he had previously facilitated the same process for a family member of one of my friends. Mehrdad, however, seemed more confident about him, repeatedly mentioning that some acquaintances had also traveled through this man's arrangements and had reached Australia safely. This was supposed to reassure me that he was trustworthy, but every time I heard this, I felt more fear.

I thought, you knew what you were getting into and were waiting for anything unusual to happen from the start." The fact that he wasn't willing to meet in public was another guarantee that he was indeed involved in this illicit business—what could almost be called a trade for him, though to me, due to my job as a commercial interpreter, the word "business" had an entirely different connotation.

Mehrdad was in constant communication with his younger brother, who was also my son's childhood friend in Australia. They both seemed very sure about this man, and they assured us after the phone call that "he is the best; he will look after you and not just take your money and vanish, like the unfortunate fate of many others." Maybe their main intention was simply to calm us down. I think they realized that since we had already begun this journey, there was no point in adding more fear and stress. Yet, if we had made the same call from Iran, I believe they would have told us to abandon this idea, advising us to forget about it entirely. One side of this endeavor was certain—death. It's not wrong to call this experience a self-willed suicide.

Or perhaps they had heard far worse stories from other travelers, which made our chosen smuggler seem like a reasonable option. There was one thing I knew for certain about myself: no one could change my mind once I had decided to do something. I wasn't as afraid of dying in the ocean as I was of going back to my old life. Now that I had come this far, there was no way back for me; if I had to return, that would be the end of my story, one way or another. I believed I had a right to my share of life—a right to enjoy freedom like anyone else. For me, freedom could not and would never be experienced in my homeland. And now, years later, I know I made the right decision through the wrong path, because that freedom remains impossible for any woman under the current government and situation.

If it wasn't my destiny to be born in a free country, where my will and choices were respected, and if, at present, I couldn't gain the freedom I deserved through normal means, then I had no other choice but to seize it the hardest way possible. If that hardest way failed, life as it was already over for me—there would be no difference then. It would be like living in a prison with only bigger walls, a life with no meaning anymore.

To follow this goal, we had no other option but to trust this stranger. Despite my overwhelming fear of the unknown journey he was preparing for us, we gave him the authority to draw the next chapter of our lives on a canvas already filled with chaos. Maybe the only thing that gave us all, those who chose this dangerous, horrific path, some courage was knowing we weren't alone. Anyway, there was no time to ponder the "what ifs" or "what if nots."

To be honest, during those moments, I feared everything and everyone, even my travel companion, my dear nephew

Meherdad. I didn't know him well either. The only thing that kept my heart warm was the sound of him calling me "aunt." That sense of familial connection was what I needed most—a reminder that someone close to me was there, that I wasn't entirely alone. Perhaps he felt the same. This young man who wouldn't stop calling me "aunt" even for a moment—it mattered to me more than to him.

For Meherdad, being young, full of hope and confidence for a bright future, was enough to keep his heart warm. He likely didn't have moments of heavy worry, or if he did, they weren't as heavy as mine. To him, it was all about the freedom to enjoy being young—a feeling I had lost long ago, even at his age. When I was his age, our days coincided with revolution and unimaginable changes, from social to financial to political—a sudden earthquake that shattered everything. Experiencing youth for my generation, victims of that revolution, meant dealing with wounds we never had the chance to heal.

The very mention of the word "smuggler" was enough to terrify an ordinary woman like me, whose most adventurous experience had been attending mixed-gender parties. In Iran, such parties—where there was music and dancing—were strictly forbidden, and the penalties enforced by the morality police were severe. None of us had ever experienced such gatherings without fear of raids, even family gatherings had strict rules: men and women were separated, or women had to cover up completely. No music, no dancing, and of course, no alcohol.

There were bans on everything—things that might seem ridiculous to those who hadn't lived this life. There were different security forces to control every aspect of society: security police, morality police. But in any dangerous or unusual situation, I knew for sure, as a woman, the last people I'd ever turn to were the police.

The man we spoke to on the phone provided us with the address of a large motel out of the city and instructed us to go there and rent a room. The motel's location was really remote and the taxi ride felt quite lengthy until we finally arrived. This distance from urban areas added to my anxiety—a motel in a remote area hardly seemed safe, especially for people like us. However, when we reached our destination, I began to understand why he had chosen such a secluded spot for our accommodation.

Upon our arrival, we found ourselves passing through a large open area with a big pool, surrounded by lots of people. There was a small café next to the pool, crowded with people too. As I listened to the conversations around me, unintentionally, I realized that most of these people were from my homeland. That's when it clicked—this was why he had picked this particular motel. It was large enough to house all these people, and it appeared that many were just like us, waiting for the next step. The pool was encircled on three sides by apartment-style buildings with three levels, and it seemed as though they were all his customers.

Without speaking to anyone, we headed straight to the reception. When we reached the desk, the staff didn't ask many questions—neither for our passports nor about how long we planned to stay. Surprisingly, our room was already booked. Seeing so many people from my country, along with the receptionist's casual approach to the check-in process, offered a strange sense of reassurance. It confirmed we had indeed come to the right place.

The receptionist handed us the room key with minimal questions, and we made our way upstairs, though I don't recall exactly which floor it was. What I do remember is that our room was tucked away behind the front door, with no sign of the large, multi-level buildings beyond.

Three buildings surrounded the spacious pool, where children played and people relaxed. Many seemed like regular tourists, but as I had initially guessed, and soon confirmed, most were in a similar situation to ours. They blended in seamlessly, with relaxed, content expressions. Seeing families gathered and children happily playing provided a strange sense of comfort. It seems that you always feel better when you have partners on the same page as you, especially in what could be considered such a crime.

We walked towards our room, navigating narrow corridors bustling with people. Many of them, clearly speaking our language, moved through the halls, making me feel a bit less isolated. The receptionist had handed us a room key, which promised at least some privacy—something I greatly valued in that moment. Given the number of people present, I wouldn't have been surprised if we'd had to stay in a communal room, which, to me, was the worst possible scenario. Our room was on an upper level and didn't resemble any hotel or motel room I had encountered before. It was a small two-bedroom suite with a compact kitchen and bathroom.

The worn-out furniture was unimpressive, but the tired ceiling fan seemed like a luxury given the rest of the room's state. The suite had two tiny, rectangular bedrooms, each with a thin double mattress covered in stained and torn sheets. Still, it was enough for me to find some solace—to lose myself in my worries and thoughts before potentially being lost in the ocean's vastness. The view from our room was nothing but neighboring rooftops. Other buildings faced ours, so close they practically touched—an arrangement that made the whole place feel like a claustrophobic grave. The worst part was those old, sagging double mattresses with dirty and ripped sheets, adding to the sense of discomfort and disrepair.

The buildings and rooftops viewed from the window gave you exactly the sense of being in a cemetery; there were no signs of life from that view. The only indication of life from the facing buildings was a few clotheslines with washed garments hanging on them. Even they looked lifeless, as if they'd been hanging there for a long time with no one coming to collect them—just like me, I thought, if I drowned in the ocean, no one would come after me either.

It might have just been laundry, but to me, it symbolized that there were other people in the neighborhood, different from the passengers in this motel—normal human beings living regular lives, not trying to escape their pasts. There was a normal life happening there, even if I couldn't see it directly.

The thought warmed my heart: strangers I couldn't see still managed to provide a sense of comfort just by hanging their laundry. Washing clothes, cooking, eating, doing the ordinary daily chores of home—all these simple acts showed that hope existed nearby. I wondered if my own laundry, hanging on a line, had ever been a symbol of hope for someone else. How desperate must that person have been? If I had known, I would have tried to hang my laundry neatly, in order to boost someone else's sense of hope.

We were still amazed while looking around that small space called a hotel room, searching around with a mixture of curiosity and disappointment. The facilities, if you could call them that, were in a sorry state. Our gaze shifted from one broken item to another as we tossed our bags onto the worn-out sofa. Meherdad sat down and mentioned that the smugglers had advised us to carry only very small bags, although we already didn't have much luggage—just the bare necessities, most of which was food.

The idea was to travel as lightly as possible so that, in case of an emergency, we could easily escape or leave our bags behind. What would you choose in such a situation? Your most valuable possessions or what could save your life? For most of us, the latter was the obvious choice. What else could you possibly think of when it came to life or death?

Later, we discovered that the restriction wasn't only about emergencies. Heavier luggage meant a greater load on the boat, and these boats could only handle so much weight. The smugglers often used worn-out boats, ones that were never intended to make a return journey—if they even reached the destination safely, which many did not, many boats sank before completing the journey. The smuggler's main goal was to maximize the number of people on board to make more deals and earn more money. He didn't care about the people on board, some of whom were very young or even newborns. I knew these boats were never meant to return to their origin; they were to be abandoned at sea. That's why they used old, worn-out boats that often broke down due to technical problems or because they were overloaded to the point of being dangerously unfit for travel. What did safety even mean in this context?

The people smugglers knew exactly who they were dealing with. Their passengers were people who had lost all hope in their home countries, people who would rather risk drowning than return to the life they were tired of. They knew these passengers would prefer death at sea to the lives they were leaving behind, or they wouldn't have started this journey at all. That was why they packed the boats as full as possible—the more desperate the people, the less they would expect from their facilitators. It was like a predator hunting its prey, forcing people into these small fishing boats. This was why so many boats never reached the Promised Land, and why so many of these poor souls, including children, lost their lives in the ocean.

Personally, I believe that if you could ask those who perished at sea and give them a voice, very few would choose to stay alive and return home instead of taking the risk for even a slight chance at a better life. It wasn't just about mere survival; it was about preserving their dignity and holding onto the pride that came with the lifestyle they chose to pursue. When we embarked on this journey, most of us thought we knew what we were getting into, but the reality was far worse than even our worst fears could have imagined.

Upon returning to our room, Meherdad expressed his desire to go downstairs near the pool to gather information from the Farsi-speaking people there. I was equally desperate for more knowledge—maybe someone downstairs could provide additional insights and help us, or at the very least help calm my worries. While he joined others around the big pool, I tried to rest, lying down on one of the worn-out mattresses with its dirty sheets and a head that felt unbearably heavy. Despite wanting so badly to rest, my mind wouldn't stop racing, and the worries wouldn't leave me alone. I turned on the TV, staring at the flickering images, though my thoughts were far away, lost in the mess of anxieties that filled my mind.

It took so long for Meherdad to come back, and when he finally returned, it was almost late afternoon. The hours of waiting had seemed endless, but when I saw him, I felt it was worth it—he was back with a wealth of information gathered from the people around the pool. It looked like my assumption had been right—all those people, and many others who were still in their rooms, were waiting for the same process to unfold. Some were even working with the same smugglers, while others were clients of different ones. Smugglers from different paths somehow worked together, and later, out of my own curiosity, I discovered why they collaborated: they all had shared connections with some powerful, corrupt officials in the Indonesian government.

This realization brought a small sense of relief, suggesting that our smuggler might not be a scammer. Of course, there was still a chance that even more terrible things could happen; bigger crimes always seemed to lurk in the shadows of desperation. However, seeing a whole group of people going through the same process gave me some solace. Regardless of what lay ahead, at least we weren't alone.

For many others, however, this motel was where their journey ended. They had handed over their money and never saw the smugglers again. Those with family support back home would reach out for more money to try a second time, but those without any support returned home empty-handed, broke, and forever marked with the blame of failure. The thought of facing such a fate—a return without anything to show—was a scenario I couldn't even imagine. To me, such an end was even worse than dying at sea.

Meherdad told me he had made some friends among the people around the pool, who had shared their stories about the journey and what we could expect next. Every piece of information mattered to us—every detail felt like it could make a difference. Comparing everything we heard from them, I had to admit that most of the stories contradict one another, only adding to my growing worries. How could there be so much contradiction about the same journey? Some people must have been exaggerating, which I understood; it was almost natural in these circumstances. We had heaps of information, but sorting through what was right and what was wrong left me feeling utterly exhausted. My mind felt like it couldn't contain all the fears, hopes, and confusion at once.

Meherdad, after collecting all that information, also seemed worn out. He ate a little, and soon after, he fell into a deep sleep. Meanwhile, I stayed up; we needed to do some shopping, and I didn't know how much longer we would be waiting to be called for boarding or even to meet the main person in charge. Sitting in front of the TV, I listened to the unfamiliar language while new thoughts and concerns swirled in my mind, all fueled by what Meherdad had said. Some of the stories he had heard seemed incredibly unbelievable, but in a situation like this—when you have no frame of reference and no experience to rely on—you find yourself giving even the most far-fetched tales a chance at being true.

When he woke up from his afternoon nap, the most ordinary part of our situation was having a cup of tea—oh, how much I missed such little pleasures. That simple act was the only aspect that felt normal, at least this one could easily be fulfilled. He seemed to enjoy making friends with the people around the pool, or perhaps he was just eager to hear more of their stories—a mix of truth and myth that fascinated both of us.

Anything was better than blindly waiting for what would happen next. He went downstairs to buy some teabags from the café near the pool. I thought he might start chatting with others again, and it would take forever for him to come back, so in a very gentle way, I asked him to come back soon. He had no real responsibility towards me, and we weren't truly family, so I had to be careful with how I spoke to him. Any misplaced words might cause misunderstanding, and I didn't want to add more stress to an already harsh situation.

He was as much a stranger to me as anyone else there, but I felt a need for his presence. I could hear voices and noises echoing through the corridor, people passing by, their voices and conversations so loud, it felt like we were in the middle of a street. No one bothered to consider the comfort or privacy of others. Still, I didn't dare open the door, even though I desperately wanted to.

Despite my request, it took him quite some time to come back. God knows how hard it was waiting in that room, staring out at nothing but the rooftops, completely alone. Every time he came back, I was eagerly waiting to hear more, and he was never without some combination of true and false information. It felt like we were playing a game of true and false, and it was up to us to guess which bits of information might actually be closer to the truth.

A few hours later, hunger got the best of me, and I opened one of the canned foods we had brought. Even with food, we had to be careful not to use it all at once. We had heard from people who had already reached Australia that it could take weeks, maybe even a month, for your turn to come. With the number of people I had seen around the pool, which seemed very likely. Aside from Meherdad's brother, we didn't have direct contact with anyone who had made it there, but we had heard these possibilities from friends and relatives, and their stories carried weight.

Although we had brought heaps of canned food to save on expenses, it wouldn't last forever—especially considering Meherdad was young, athletic, and needed to eat well. The food was cold and tasted horrible, but like every other unpleasant thing we endured in those moments, I kept repeating in my head, "It's okay, it's temporary. Wait, good things will happen after." I tried not to dwell on it too much, because having delicious, warm food was the least of my worries at that point. As long as it killed my hunger and filled my stomach, it was enough.

When twilight came, Meherdad returned to his new friends by the pool. I was longing for that cup of tea, but I didn't even ask about it. I had already given him the money for it, but like so many other things, I decided to let it go. He started narrating what he had heard from the people he met, and I focused instead on listening to those stories, feeling a sense of relief that, in such a short period, he had made many friends.

The stories he shared painted a picture of the journey as carefree, as if we were embarking on a five-star cruise. There was nothing to worry about, according to them. Deep down, I knew that couldn't be true, but I wanted to pretend I believed him. Part of it was to make Meherdad happy, and part of it was to calm my own anxious thoughts, to trick my mind into believing everything would be just fine.

Chapter Six

Meherdad continued talking when, suddenly, the door swung open—as I should have expected. No warning, no permission, not even a knock to see whether we were ready for them or not. A young couple entered, led by another young man who was instructing them that this was going to be their room too. He was clearly one of those working for the smuggler.

Although I didn't like my privacy being invaded, I wasn't entirely unhappy to see them. The young man explained that the smugglers had arranged for the couple to stay in our spare room. Later, I learned this was a common practice—people were constantly being moved around to new rooms or places with little to no notice.

The surprise must have been clear on my face, and I kept reminding myself that this wasn't like any other trip I had ever taken. The concept of privacy had no place here, and I thought to myself that this man had no obligation to ask for our permission before bringing strangers into our space. It was an unsettling reminder of the situation we were in, a stark contrast to anything resembling normal travel.

I and Meherdad tried to get some more information from the young man, thinking that since he worked for the smuggler, his information might be more accurate. However, it was useless; he was accustomed to these actions and gave us little in terms of insight. Those like him, for various reasons—sometimes the misfortune of lacking money—had ended up working for smugglers to earn enough for their own journeys or, in exchange for working for the smugglers for some time, would eventually be transferred themselves.

The young couple had only been married for a few months, and it was obvious that the girl, Zara, wasn't happy at all about her husband's decision to take on this dangerous journey. She wore a bit-ter expression, a permanent frown on her face. Her husband, Mohammad, on the other hand, was relentless in his chatter—he spoke endlessly about his profession as a welder and how his wife, being a nurse, would be in high demand in Australia. He was sure that a bright future awaited them in that Promised Land. It seemed like his constant talking was an attempt to convince his wife that he had made the right choice. He painted a vivid picture of companies begging him to work with them.

To be honest, that chatterbox was exactly what I needed that night. Doubts about the decision we had made haunted us all, even those of us pretending otherwise, and having a "partner in crime" was probably the best thing that could happen in such circumstances. In any normal situation, I would have tried to look busy to avoid their conversation, but at that moment, I pretended, with eager eyes, that I enjoyed hearing his dreams. I really needed someone to talk to, even if his words were nonsense. In reality, we weren't even his true audience—his main listener was his wife, Zara.

With her frowning face, Zara listened to him with one eye on us, observing our reactions to his words. He was clearly painting this dream canvas for her, trying desperately to win her over, hoping for her agreement, but from the expression she wore, you could easily tell it wouldn't be that simple. She was unconvinced, her doubts written across her face, while Mohammad continued his optimistic rambling, trying to bridge the gap between their hopes and their harsh reality.

He was so busy with his own details and the story of how he and his wife would successfully end up settling in Australia that he didn't give us any chance to speak at all. I didn't mind this and actually preferred him to keep going. I wasn't as good as he was at dreaming of future days I wasn't sure would ever come. After a while, when he seemed to tire of talking so much, he decided to take a rest and started asking about us—our plans, how we ended up there, and how we had found out about this particular smuggler. I really didn't want to discuss this subject at all, not just because I didn't want to share information with a stranger, especially when we were in such a precarious situation, but also because I simply wasn't in the mood to discuss something so uncertain.

Frankly, I wasn't in the mood to talk about anything. Listening, even pretending to listen, was far more comfortable—it let my mind drift elsewhere. I felt too stressed and depleted to engage in any meaningful conversation. I made my answers as brief as possible, and anyone paying attention could have seen that I was unwilling. He must have noticed because, after a while, his tone shifted. He seemed a bit arrogant and started comparing his talents with ours, even though he barely knew us. It wasn't important to me at all; we might never see him again after a day or two, so let him talk about his qualities and talents as much as he wanted, if it boosted his ego. I didn't care if my minimal answers made him feel superior, thinking that he was more useful, a more deserving citizen of Australia compared to us. Australia, oh, what a dream.

Perhaps he was underestimating me because I was much older than most of them. In truth, almost all the other passengers I met later were much younger, except for a few. Many times, I saw it in their faces, even if they didn't say it outright: what was I doing here at this age? Their expressions, whether openly or subtly, questioned my presence. It happened so often that I even began to lose my confidence. But as time went on, life played other games with me—whether it was luck, resilience, or destiny, I managed to continue on, even if those dreams had been distant for years.

When he realized I wasn't interested in being his conversation partner, he took it upon himself to continue talking. I was grateful he was so understanding, especially on this particular topic. He talked non-stop, and his beautiful wife tried in various ways to remind him to keep quiet. The entire time, I had a feeling that she wasn't enjoying her husband's performance. However, she chose to stay silent, probably to avoid escalating his chatter into an unnecessary argument. From his words, it was clear that she wasn't the decision-maker here—she was following, like many Persian women often did.

It was a few hours after sunset. Though the charm of listening to him had worn off, it was still better than being alone in that ugly, worn-out room. I preferred their company over sitting alone in that dreadful space. I suggested that we have dinner, and we set a small table. We shared what we had, opening a few cans and warming up the food as best we could. After dinner, Meherdad announced that he wanted to go out with a new friend he had just met. The man wanted to join them too but chose to stay behind so his wife wouldn't be left alone. From his demeanor, I realized that, despite all his confident words, he was just as worried as the rest of us. He tried to hide it for his wife's sake, but his unease showed.

When Meherdad left, I suggested that we get some rest. I knew that as soon as Meherdad left, the man would likely find more topics to talk about, and I wasn't ready for that. So, I recommended resting, and thankfully, he agreed. His wife and I went to one of the rooms while the men took the other. Surprisingly, I fell asleep right away. I lost track of time, and before I knew it, I had no idea when Meherdad returned.

Although this constant feeling of being worried seemed never-ending, feeling tired—whether from a long, exhausting day or because of the talkative man next to us—was actually not that bad after all, and it let me have a long and deep sleep. It's funny how pillows, as soon as you rest your head on them, seem to invite all the worries of the world to attack you. But maybe I was lucky because this pillow was so uncomfortable that it actually distracted my mind from those constant fears. I couldn't help but remember how unbearably uncomfortable my neck felt with that pillow, as hard as a rock beneath my head.

Those worn-out and highly uncomfortable mattresses were stronger than my anxiety. I don't know about the young woman, but the next morning, I found out that they all also had a deep sleep. A simple breakfast table was set, and the young man, surprisingly, was not as eager to talk as he had been the night before. While we were eating, the couple received a call—maybe from the smuggler—and left in a rush without any explanation. We didn't bother asking any questions either; we all accepted that this was how things went in such an unpredictable journey.

Soon after, Meherdad also received a call from the smugglers. They told him they would meet us later, either in the late afternoon or early evening, but no specific time was given for the meeting. That lack of certainty was obvious; everything, even the smallest details, had to remain secret. He mentioned that he would drop by sometime during the day, but not at an exact hour. I was genuinely curious to meet him. Part of that curiosity was an expectation that he would look different from ordinary people. To me, a smuggler should look like something from a movie—a huge man with lots of hair, dark, maybe with scars on his face and a strange, deep voice.

He advised us not to leave the room, so I stayed in that hot, muggy space all day. Meherdad, however, did not care about the instructions as much and soon left, saying he would come back shortly. I took advantage of this and asked him to do some shopping for the things we needed, giving him money again. Although it was difficult for me to stay alone all the time, I could understand his restlessness. Staying in such a room—small, dirty, with no one to talk to and little to do—was too boring for a young man like Meherdad. It was boring for me too, but with more experience, I knew how to be patient when necessary.

After the smuggler's call, he tried to stay in the room a bit longer, but he got bored easily and couldn't stand it anymore. He left to mingle with the people around the pool downstairs. I really wished he would follow the smuggler's advice because we only had one cell phone, and I wouldn't be able to inform him if the smuggler suddenly showed up. Besides, I didn't know what kind of people we were dealing with. Part of me wanted Meherdad to stay, but I knew I could not—and should not—expect him to listen to me. So, I kept silent and stayed in the room, hoping the smuggler would come by when Meherdad was also there.

Later, I learned that the smuggler could easily call on him, even when he was out of the motel, because he had people working for him all over the city. He could find anyone he wanted, anytime. Personally, this realization wasn't very reassuring. What kind of operation needs such a big network? If he required such a large number of people working under him, then they were probably dealing with very dangerous things too.

I could hear many people talking and passing through the corridors. They seemed to be living their normal lives, as I could understand from their conversations. Some were speaking loudly about this journey. It seemed like I was the only one hesitating to talk about it, which was ironic since we were all here for the same reason. Why was I so hesitant to speak about it?

Part of it may have come from the constant fear that the ruling government had injected into every cell of us—especially in me, who had been a citizen since the beginning of the revolution, almost from the first month when this regime of fear took hold. As all the others were much younger than me. When you are young, you don't take danger as seriously. With the confidence that comes from inexperience, you think you are capable of overcoming any dangerous situation.

The smuggler didn't show up until late afternoon, and thank God, Meherdad had returned by then. When he came back, he reassured me that the smuggler wouldn't arrive until either the evening or late afternoon, thanks to his new friends who had given him this information, among many other details—some believable, some unbelievable. It was a blessing to hear these updates; I was as thirsty as he was to learn more. Even the smallest piece of information helped me put together another fragment of the unclear puzzle in my head. What else could we rely on for now? I don't think it was just me; everyone here shared the same interest.

It was late afternoon, and we were both waiting in our room, staring at the TV to kill time. Suddenly, the door opened—as usual, without a knock or any permission to enter, something we had grown used to by now. My wide-open eyes revealed a tall, middle-aged man, perhaps in his 40s, with an almost skinny build and a face not too dark. A big, thick black beard covered his entire face—you could hardly guess what he might look like if he shaved. He was wearing a sports hat, which added further cover to his face, and a casual, somewhat worn-out outfit. A young man accompanied him; I had seen him in the corridor before but not with this man. The moment they stepped into the room, I knew he must be the one—they called him Boby. From how he was treated by others and his own bossy attitude, you could easily see that those around him were obedient, whether out of fear or for money.

He looked completely different from what I had expected. I had imagined someone huge, muscular, with tattoos covering his body, and a big, scarred face. He was nothing like that. On the contrary, he looked quite ordinary. If I had met him somewhere else, I would never have imagined him to be involved in such activities. Maybe too many movies had shaped my expectations about smugglers—painting an image far from reality.

This was no movie; even the most innocent faces could hide something far more sinister, or vice versa. Even though he was sitting close to us in that small room, I could hardly see him clearly. The beard, with its overwhelming amount of hair, and the hat covered almost all of his face, barely giving me a chance to imagine how he might look without them. Besides, the room's lighting was insufficient—strangely, it was only then that I noticed how dim the light in the room truly was.

His beard was so thick and abundant that it crossed my mind that maybe it was fake. As I stared at him with obvious curiosity, I thought that if I ever saw him somewhere without the beard and hat, I would never recognize him. It was quite understandable that he chose this appearance for himself deliberately. The lighting was also poor—an old bulb with a faded glow did not allow me to make out the details of his face perfectly. And, of course, part of my difficulty in seeing clearly was due to the stress, making it hard to concentrate.

Yet, there was something unmistakably unique about him—his strong and rough voice. Since I was so curious to discover more about him, I listened carefully to the tone and tried to commit it to memory. Even now, I can still hear his voice in my ears.

Despite all the stress and worry, I couldn't help but want to learn more about his character. What kind of person would get involved in such a task? Was he stupid, greedy, corrupted, smart, or something else? I realized it was probably a bit of all these things. I just wanted to remember something about him to test my recognition skills if life ever gave me another chance to meet him in a different situation. I wanted something to help me recognize him, and his distinct voice was the perfect clue—especially for someone in his late 40s, without even a single gray hair in that massive beard. I wasn't wrong about guessing his age, and that voice confirmed it. A young man like Meherdad could never have had such a mature tone.

He asked about us—our jobs, where we used to live, and how many kids I had—and the same questions were asked of Meherdad. He continued by explaining that there was no clear date or time for the day we would set sail, as this was not a normal way of traveling. Even if he knew in advance, he would never inform the passengers, and for security reasons, he always kept it secret. "If the Indonesian police find out," he warned, "we would all end up in jail, and only those who have enough money to bribe them would have a second chance." Luck had nothing to do with this situation; only money could solve a problem like that.

He continued, saying that we needed to be ready all the time—he might even come to our door in an hour and ask us to join the group and leave immediately. That's why he advised us to stay in the motel as much as possible. It seemed like he had given the same advice to everyone, but I could see others constantly coming and going, which made me think either he was exaggerating or others simply weren't taking his warnings seriously.

He asked us to show him our luggage. Although we each only had a small bag, he said we were carrying too much. He advised us to make our luggage as light as possible and also explained what kind of food we were allowed to have with us, which we already knew thanks to Meherdad's brother and his new friends around the pool. They also suggested that we wrap all our documents, clothes, and food in plastic wrap in case of water penetration—so our belongings wouldn't get wet. I must say, this was the best advice we had received, especially considering the harsh storms we would later face. It felt like we were almost inside the water.

Finally, he started talking about the price. He mentioned that the standard cost ranged between $5,000 and $6,000 per person. But then, pointing at me, he said, "You look like my mom, and I haven't seen my mom in a long time, so I'll charge each of you $4,800." I couldn't trust him entirely, but when I met the others on the boat, I found out he had given each of us different prices, and it turned out the amount he charged us was actually better compared to others.

He also kept calling me "auntie," just as Meherdad did, and this continued throughout the entire journey. Everyone else started calling me "auntie" too, which I didn't mind at all. Even today, so many years later, if I run into any of them by accident, they still call me "auntie." That's how I became Auntie to the entire Iranian community in Australia, a title that has lasted until today. We gave him our money, hands shaking slightly—there was no guarantee when trusting this complete stranger, whose real name we didn't even know.

He then gave us some information about the boat we were going to travel on, assuring us that it would be a safe boat, not a wreck. He emphasized that none of the people who worked with him had ever drowned, and those who had faced such a fate had worked with other smugglers. It was unbelievable, of course, and if I had asked other smugglers, they probably would have said the exact same thing about him.

He mentioned that he needed to leave that evening to meet another family, but there were always men working for him here at the motel, and he would make the next contact through them. As he was leaving the room, I overheard another man in the corridor call him by a different name—and this happened many times, each time with a new name. Later, when we started the journey on the boat, I asked a few other passengers why he had a different name for different people. I learned that by doing so, he categorized his passengers, perhaps by age or by the money he charged each person. It seemed he had really charged us differently, and why was that only he could answer.

Maybe he felt sorry for those in more difficult financial situations—perhaps that was why he asked about our jobs and where we used to live. Whatever his reasons were, when I found out that he had indeed charged us less than others, I felt ashamed for accusing him of lying. Maybe I really did remind him of his mother. Everyone has a heart, even those we expect not to, but our interpretations are often skewed because we need proof of evil in order to justify our judgment and punishment.

He also said we would be setting sail soon, maybe even this week, but not later. This was good news—the sooner, the better—which made us happy. We knew that there were people who had been waiting for months for their turn, and I wondered what his priority was for sending people out. Was it the amount of money they paid? It was all in his hands, and only he could decide who would leave first.

Now that we knew we would be leaving soon, we felt a bit more relaxed. We decided to go outside and do some shopping—food was at the top of our list. We needed provisions for the next few days as well as during the journey, plus some medicine just in case. I already had sunscreen, a hat, and so on, but there were other necessities we had recently been advised to get: medicine, vitamins, plastic wrap and other necessities.

Chapter Seven

As we passed through the corridor, we overheard people talking. We learned that a boat had hit the ocean just a day before and was about to sink. All the passengers had survived because it broke apart before getting too far out into the ocean, and they had just returned to the motel.

Everyone else around the pool was talking about the new arrivals, and we were also curious to see them, hoping to gather more information from them. Meherdad said that after we returned from shopping, he would go and find out more about them.

The shops were not as large or glamorous as those I had seen in other countries I had visited, but they were still interesting enough for wandering around. We went and bought some supplies, and one of the most important was anti-nausea medication—just in case we got seasick. How had I not thought about it before? I had never experienced sea sailing, and there was a good chance it could affect me quite badly. Although I felt somewhat more relaxed compared to our arrival that constant feeling of worry remained. It wasn't as intense as the first day, but it was still there. Maybe the meeting with the smuggler and the assurance that the process would soon begin had helped, or perhaps it was because I thought I should hold myself together as the older and more experienced one, someone with responsibilities. That was why, until the last day, I pretended that everything was fine—that I was enjoying our time in front of Meherdad. In reality, I doubted he cared much.

It might sound funny, but I wasn't acting out of obligation. I genuinely cared about him as my dear nephew, and I felt a sense of duty to look after him. In our last moments before saying goodbye, his father had entrusted him to me. I didn't want to burden him by showing how worried I was or talking about my constant anxiety. It seemed he wasn't as concerned as I expected anyway.

A few times, when Meherdad went out, I decided to join others at the small café, which seemed like the most luxurious part of this trip, as funny as that sounds. Its plastic chairs—at most, ten of them—stood around a very small counter with a tiny commercial fridge. It wasn't much of a luxury, but it was better than nothing. Despite being called a café, all they served were tea bags, instant coffee, some fruits, cold and hot soft drinks, and biscuits, but a large number of people still gathered around it.

Some people came and sat next to me, starting conversations and even asking personal questions, which I really didn't want to answer. One amusing bit of information I gathered was that most of them claimed to be from Tehran, specifically from one downtown suburb. I knew that area very well, and from the news in Iran, I had always heard that it was a difficult place to live—full of crime and criminals. That fact added to my fears.

Later, when we were on the boat, a young boy told me that many of them just pretended to be from that suburb. In reality, some were from regional and remote villages. I couldn't understand why they would want to boast about being from such a place, and when I asked, he explained that the reputation of that area gave the impression they were tough and not easily scammed or ripped off. I couldn't disagree more—this kind of thinking was beyond my understanding, yet it made sense to many of them. During the entire journey, I heard several of them proudly announcing that they came from that specific part of the capital.

Regardless of their attitudes or beliefs, their presence was a blessing to me. Even if I didn't speak much with them, I was thankful they were there. I did not want to go back to my room; sitting in that space with nothing but a view of rooftops was unbearable. It reminded me of a cemetery, and in our room, I was alone most of the time. At least here, I could see some faces, and that was more comforting than the solitude of the room.

I left the motel a few times without Meherdad, as he was often hard to find. I wasn't afraid of going out on my own—this wasn't my first time overseas, and I had traveled alone many times before. However, I didn't venture far from the motel. My fair and blonde hair worked in my favor, allowing me to pass off as European, and maybe that could keep me safer. My appearance, after all, was entirely different from that of the locals.

Even if someone did start a conversation, I avoided revealing my country of origin. Firstly, because I knew that if I did, they would immediately know why I was at this motel, and I disliked the vulnerability of that knowledge. Secondly, in many parts of the world, there is an understanding that Western-style countries will have embassies that stand firmly behind their citizens in case of trouble. But for us, there was no such backing. If I ended up needing my embassy, it would only lead to more problems for me, not less.

But to my surprise, I found that the local people treated us fairly. Not just with me, but also with those less cautious than I was. Even more astonishing was the fact that they didn't seem to mind or even care about us being there. With the large number of people like us—all from the same country—they could have easily reported us to the police or at least questioned our presence. Why didn't they? Later, I learned that smugglers had their own spies within the police, and the one we were dealing with was one of the major players. In fact, through a certain incident, I even ended up speaking with the "big boss" on the phone, as I was the only one among us who could speak English.

Going out was a blessing, even if I didn't venture far or stay out for long. Those few opportunities to step outside gave me a chance to observe the bustling, crowded city and its people. It was a kind of escape. As I watched passers-by living their normal lives, I felt a sense of sadness, both for myself and for everyone else in our group. Each of us had our reasons for choosing this unusual path of migration. Of course, no one would prefer this, but somehow, we all reached a point where we believed this was the best option for us, regardless of the outcome.

I couldn't help but reflect on how, not too long ago, I too had lived a normal life, unaware that my world would take such a turn. I wished I could linger outside a bit longer, escaping the constant burden of overthinking. But I chose to remain cautious, to not push my luck. Going back to that room was undesirable; everything about it felt repulsive—especially my own emotions. The stress and uncertainty I felt seemed to seep into the room itself, and I found myself irrationally blaming it for my situation. This made enduring the ordeal even harder, and I had no idea how much longer I'd be stuck there—although, in a surprising twist, it wasn't for as long as I had feared.

When I was alone in the room, I had nothing to entertain myself with except the words I'd heard about our journey, whether from other passengers in the motel or from the smuggler himself. There were similarities and contradictions in what they said, and although I couldn't trust which side was telling the truth, it was still better than knowing nothing at all.

Sometimes, I tried to keep myself busy by cooking with the few ingredients I bought from local shops. Meherdad usually ate outside with his friends, and I was left alone for lunch or dinner. It was even more boring to eat by myself, so I decided to stop cooking and eat out too. However, a few times when I bought food from local restaurants or street booths, the taste or the food itself didn't sit well with me—it caused some health trouble, and that was why I eventually returned to cooking in the room.

The short conversation we had with the smuggler stayed in the back of my mind, and I kept reviewing every word he said, hoping to uncover even the smallest sign or piece of information about our journey. I constantly went over the requirements, the terms and conditions, and the necessary items and tasks. These requirements were, without a doubt, rules that he himself had concocted. People like him set their own rules for such journeys, leaving no room for objections or debate, regardless of logic. It was a simple choice—comply or don't come.

I pondered whether embarking on this trip would bring me the freedom I yearned for in my life or if it would just end in a superficial change without true liberation. Sadly, I found my answer as the journey not only began but also concluded, in every possible way. If I were to compare what he was doing and offering to any other business, in a normal situation, we as buyers would never let the seller impose all these rules and obligations on us. But this was not a normal business; it was something illegal, something conducted in the shadows.

His rules dictated that we hand over our money, essentially our lives, in exchange for this treacherous and unconventional means of transportation. Losing our money would be hard, but ultimately, it was replaceable. Our lives, however, were not. Still, neither I nor the others wanted this life if we couldn't live it the way we wanted to—if we had to keep pretending, and couldn't dare to be ourselves.

So, I accepted his bullying attitude and ridiculous rules, with the hope that this would be the last time someone dictated to me what to do in the simple matters of my life. I hoped, more than anything, that this was the final time. But on the other hand, there was no guarantee that this journey would lead to the paradise I had envisioned. What if he turned out to be a scammer like so many others? With the little money I had left, I wouldn't last long. I knew it would be foolish to ask for any kind of receipt or proof of payment for this risky and unconventional method of transfer—who in their right mind would ask for a guarantee from a human trafficker?

I had no illusions about the absurdity of my situation. After all, who could be naïve enough to ask someone involved in smuggling to guarantee a positive outcome? In what world could anyone expect a receipt from someone who deals in human lives? It was just one of the many compromises I had to make, holding onto the thin hope that this would somehow lead me to the freedom I craved.

I felt a kind of jealousy towards everyone else I met in that motel; it seemed like I was the only one unable to enjoy the time there. Going out more often helped me to embrace the role of a traveler, rather than a perpetually worried passenger. I wished I at least had a few books with me to read, though with my low level of concentration, I doubted it would have made much difference.

Everyone else around the pool looked more like carefree travelers, which surprised me—they seemed like they were on holiday, sitting comfortably (or at least pretending to) on those plastic, uncomfortable chairs at the café. I decided to make one more attempt to join the others at that small café. I ventured over to the pool area and ordered a coffee—it might not have been real coffee, but it was good enough to satisfy my craving. Finding an unoccupied table was a bit of a challenge due to the crowd, but eventually, I found one by the pool. I sat down, watching children happily swim, completely unaware of the decisions their parents had made for them.

While most of the people around the pool looked relaxed and content, I found some momentary peace in this scene. This decision to stay there worked for the moment, keeping me seated for hours. I saw both new and familiar faces from previous days, and it seemed like new arrivals were happening constantly. A young man eventually sat next to me without asking for permission, which was very common here. He didn't ask me why I was there—he already knew what brought us all to this place. Instead, he asked, "Are you also after a better life?" I didn't know how to answer. Part of me didn't want to continue the conversation in this direction, while another part was tired of staying quiet. I decided to try steering the conversation elsewhere, but it didn't work—there was no other interesting subject for these people except the journey ahead and when it would be their turn to hit the ocean.

Another tactic I tried was answering his questions with my own, like where he was from, what his job was, and how long he had been there. This approach worked well, as it turned out people loved talking about themselves. It was fascinating—all those I spoke to, even later, seemed convinced they would become the most useful citizens once they arrived in Australia. They believed that the country would need their skills, even those who had no profession were planning their bright futures. It looked like I was the only one doubting her future, despite being able to communicate verbally and connect more easily.

I wasn't sure if this lack of confidence was due to my age, inadequate self-development, or maybe because I had experienced life in a Western country and knew it wouldn't be as easy as they imagined. Whatever the cause, it prevented me from enjoying the situation as much as the others seemed to. On the other hand, perhaps it was a good sign—it made me act more cautiously. But in a harsh moment, like God forbid, if we were to drown in the ocean, what good would caution do for any of us?

I could easily see that Meherdad was enjoying himself, much like everyone else around the pool. For most of them, this was their first international trip, and for those I chatted with, it was clear that none had traveled abroad before. It piqued their interest and filled them with excitement, but for me, it was just another excursion, without the glamor and luxury associated with typical trips. Instead, this journey was filled with uncertainty and fear.

Most of these travelers were young, born during or shortly after the Iranian Revolution in 1978. The revolution had stripped away many basic rights, including the freedom to enjoy life's simple pleasures. Seeing women walk freely without veils or enjoying a glass of beer had become symbols of an unattainable paradise. To them, these were dreams, mere glimpses of what life could have been, and now they were hoping to make those dreams a reality.

These distractions were sufficient to overshadow the perils that awaited everyone on this trip. I could scarcely find anyone my age, and if there were any, they weren't from my country, at least while I was at the motel. Later, I met a few, but even they were some years younger than me.

Talking to that man in the café did its job in distracting my mind. When Meherdad returned from exploring the city with his new friends, I could easily see signs of surprise on his face when he found me downstairs, mingling with the crowd around the pool. He must have thought to himself that his constantly worried Auntie was finally behaving like everyone else. It seemed strange to him that I would be so concerned about what lay ahead, but perhaps it was for the same reason I mentioned earlier—a reason that clearly had no meaning for him.

I saw many kids around the pool, accompanied by their parents. If all these people were in the same situation as us, then these children would be traveling with them. I couldn't decide whether to call it courage or recklessness—to allow such little children to face a dangerous situation like this. Or maybe it's not fair for me to judge them; after all, I didn't know their story. What must they have endured to accept such a risk, not just for themselves but for their children as well?

I had been sitting and mingling with others around the pool for almost a few hours. It was amazing how time flew when you were around others, even those with whom you had nothing in common except one shared, final solution: the willingness to risk your life. Perhaps that alone was enough—we were all risking the most precious thing we had, our lives.

I asked Meherdad if he was hungry, and we ascended to our room together, feeling the need to eat. I heated up one of the canned foods we had brought, and as we ate, Meherdad eagerly shared more information he had gathered from others. I was always happy to hear anything new and grateful that he was so generous in sharing every little piece of information he got. He spoke of some strange situations we should expect. According to what he had heard, some had already attempted the boat journey, only for their vessel to break down after a few hours, forcing them to return and wait for another opportunity.

To me, that meant the boats were even worse than the smuggler had promised us. They should consider themselves lucky it broke down only a few hours into the journey; had it been further out, they could all have drowned. I remembered hearing earlier from someone that one of the broken boats' passengers had just come back. They all survived, but they returned to the motel in a terrible state.

Meherdad recounted how some of them had claimed it wasn't difficult at all, and expressed their excitement to set sail once again. I couldn't understand how anyone could be so thrilled about such an uncomfortable and perilous mode of travel. Some of the details Meherdad relayed seemed questionable to me, but for some reason, he was inclined to believe them. Not wanting to dampen his spirits, I pretended to believe them too.

Maybe this was his way of coping with fear and stress—escaping reality until the inevitable moment of reckoning arrived. After all, we all sometimes act this way, choosing to pretend everything is fine instead of facing problems head-on. Whatever his reason, I didn't want to, and obviously couldn't, convince him otherwise. Pretending everything was easy and normal might be a way to cope, but to me, it came across as carelessness, and that worried me deeply.

Nonetheless, it was always enjoyable and captivating to listen to Meherdad's stories, whether they were rooted in reality or just his own fabrications. Speculating about the potential intricacies of this journey became the most engaging topic of conversation—not just for me and him, but for everyone around us. After lunch, Meherdad took a nap while I sat in front of the TV, mulling over his words, trying to distinguish what could be real from what was merely imagined by him or his friends. How I wished I could sleep too, but I knew myself too well—the moment my head touched the pillow, all the negative thoughts would invade my mind.

While my eyes were fixed on the TV screen, my thoughts drifted through everything Meherdad had said. Suddenly, we heard a forceful knock on the door. Startled, Meherdad and I exchanged glances, as we hadn't anticipated any visitors. Clearly, this unexpected and harsh knock could only mean one thing: it must be the smuggler's notice for leaving.

Meherdad hastily opened the door, and there stood a man before us, his voice loud and far from pleasant. He inquired about where we had been, falsely claiming to have been waiting for us for some time. I suppose he wanted to establish his dominance—something shallow people often do when given the chance to be the center of attention. Another man joined him, sharing some information about someone they both seemed to know. It became clear to us that they were both working for the smuggler, as it seemed he had an extensive team in place.

With an unpleasant harshness in his voice, the man finally declared, "Be ready. You are boarding tonight." We were completely caught off guard. No further notice, no explanation—just an expectation to comply. After all, this journey required us to be on standby, always prepared. What else could we have expected?

Both Meherdad and I were overwhelmed with stress. For the first time, Meherdad stopped pretending to be so calm. Perhaps there were some preparations we needed to make, but there was nothing we could really do except wait for the smuggler's staff to come back with further instructions. Our bags were already packed, made lighter from finishing most of the food we had brought. I thought maybe we should replace some of it, but we needed to keep everything as light as possible.

I went downstairs to the café to buy some fruit, thinking it might be the best option to eat on the boat if we got seasick. I already had some medicines and sour candies, unsure of how my body would react to the sea's constant motion, especially with such a boat—it would be much harsher. I had never experienced being on a boat, and if seasickness hit me, it would double the disaster, something none of us needed.

When I returned to the room, Meherdad was nowhere to be found. The man had explicitly told us to stay in our room, as he could show up at any moment to announce it was time. Oh, this boy was getting on my nerves, treating this entire trip as if he were embarking on a luxurious five-star cruise. Perhaps he had gone to say goodbye to his new friends, but it never once crossed my mind that I could leave without him. Like a dear child, I wanted him with me everywhere I went, as if his presence alone provided a sense of security and comfort I desperately needed.

Chapter Eight

With no other choice but to wait for Meherdad in the room, I was careful not to say anything that might upset him. It took a few hours for Meherdad to return, and thank God he made it back before the smuggler's staff showed up.

In the late afternoon, as the sky darkened, the angry man knocked on our door again. At least he knocked, instead of barging in suddenly like others had done before. His voice was loud and commanding, with the tone of a commander addressing his soldiers. He instructed us to come upstairs to another room—room number 10. We immediately left our room, moving to the new location he had assigned. The room was filled with people, a big group that included families and singles. It was almost too many for one room.

He explained that, to avoid arousing suspicion from the Indonesian police—who were actively searching for people like us—it would be better for Meherdad and I to be separated temporarily. Meherdad was sent to join the group of singles, while I was placed among a group of families. To my surprise, I actually preferred this, as it made me feel more comfortable. The smuggler's staff then outlined the plan to us: we would be traveling to the airport in smaller groups, boarding different planes to avoid drawing attention. If a large group of us boarded the same flight, it would be obvious, from our appearance, our gestures, and the language we spoke, that we were all from the same place.

Once we reached the nearest state to the shores, where the boat was docked, we would be taken by bus from the airport to the forest near the coast, where the boat awaited. He assured me that I would meet up with Meherdad there. It was better, he said, for us to start the journey separately. Meherdad left the room with the other young men, and among everyone in that crowded space, I only recognized the young couple who had spent a night in our room before. I never imagined that seeing them again would bring me such relief. The girl sat next to me with a big smile and called me "Auntie," saying, "How good it is that you are with us." It made me feel reassured.

The singles, including Meherdad, left first in groups. The angry man asked us to wait, as a taxi was ready for the first group at the front door. Each group, about eight to ten people, left in intervals of 10-15 minutes. He explained that this was done to avoid drawing too much attention from the neighbors or passersby—especially those who could be spies for the police. I suppose they meant those who hadn't yet been bribed. After a while, it was the families' turn to leave, one group at a time.

When it was my group's turn, taxis were waiting for us at the front door to take us to the airport. It seemed even the taxi drivers knew their role in this operation. The angry man instructed us to scatter and not mingle with each other once we reached the airport. As we arrived, I noticed some familiar faces from the pool area, including a young woman named Rema and her little daughter, who was about three years old. Rema caught my attention because of her loud voice and her apparent lack of concern for her daughter's safety. Even back at the pool, she never seemed to worry about the child, often letting her wander while she chatted with others.

Rema was young and beautiful, and her carefree attitude seemed to attract men easily—something she was clearly aware of. I had often seen her at the café, mingling with different men and even asking them to buy things for her and her daughter. Though it wasn't my business, her behavior made me uncomfortable, and I hoped she wouldn't end up in my group. Unfortunately, she did. She sat beside me in the taxi, and at the airport, she stuck close to me, calling me "Mommy" from the very beginning, trying to win me over in her own way. Though her manipulative behavior was clear, I kept quiet for the sake of her little girl, and I was sure the men around us were doing the same for similar reasons.

The taxi passed through the streets, and I preferred to look out at the surroundings, though her incessant chatter was distracting. Finally, we arrived at the local airport. It wasn't large or luxurious, but who cared about that at the time? I saw the other groups, but not the one with Meherdad. I tried to follow the instructions we had been given—not to make ourselves too noticeable. Meanwhile, Rema continued her loud, attention-seeking behavior. Her voice, her striking appearance, and her daughter wandering around with no supervision drew too much attention for my liking.

I felt a growing anger at her disregard for the situation and our safety. Still, I kept silent—I didn't want an argument, especially not in such a fragile moment. Besides, seeing her daughter cry for water tugged at my heart, and I ended up helping her despite my irritation. I really didn't appreciate Rema's sudden familiarity, and mainly because her behavior put us all at risk. There was also something suspicious about her friendliness. When I bought water for the girl, I prayed Rema wouldn't end up next to me on the plane. Fortunately, once we boarded, she seemed to realize I wasn't an easy mark and left me alone, choosing to engage others instead.

Once we disembarked, an Asian-looking man approached us, claiming to be from the smuggler. He used the secret signs and words the smuggler had told us to expect, and it seemed he was legitimate. It was dark outside when we left the airport, adding to the sense of mystery. The airport itself was in a remote area, with little lighting around. He led us to a small minibus, where I saw some other members of our group already waiting—nine people, including the driver. There must have been other vans taking the rest of us.

As soon as I sat down, the van began moving towards an unknown destination. None of us knew where we were going, and the driver only smiled whenever we asked questions, offering no answers. It was understandable—he couldn't speak English, and I didn't know why others kept asking me to translate when it was clear communication wasn't possible. We continued driving silently through the night, the driver's smile our only form of interaction. It was almost midnight by then, and everything was closed.

Each of us in the van had different scenarios playing out in our minds. I, too, had my fears, but I kept them to myself, unlike the chatterbox man beside me, who insisted we were being driven to a remote area to be killed and have our organs sold.

The longer the driver continued on these unfamiliar roads, the more convinced this man became of his gruesome theory. I was deeply scared myself, but I couldn't understand why the smuggler would go to such lengths just to kill us—buying plane tickets, taking us to another state. Surely, if he wanted to get rid of us, there were easier and closer ways. I shared my thoughts, but the man dismissed me, referring to some movie he had seen. The driver took us through dark, winding roads until we reached an area so remote there was no sign of civilization—just thick darkness and endless trees.

When he finally pointed for us to get out, we felt utterly lost—left in the middle of nowhere. In those moments, I couldn't help but wonder if, after all, the chatterbox man's grim predictions might be true. In situations like these, fear makes even the most terrible ideas seem possible.

The passengers were mostly young, although I couldn't see their faces clearly from my seat. I could sense their fear in their voices, even as they chattered nonstop, speculating about where we were. While I remained quiet, listening to them, they seemed to grow more nervous. The driver glanced at us occasionally with a strange smile—it was hard to tell if it was meant to be friendly or if there was something darker behind it. Whatever the case, it certainly wasn't comforting. He knew what he was doing, but we couldn't decipher its meaning—only feel its impact. In moments like this, any unknown factor only added to our fear, as the unknown often does in life.

The driver got out of the van, opened the sliding door, and pointed for us to exit. We were understandably afraid, hesitant to step into an unfamiliar, dark place. The chatterbox boy continued advising everyone not to listen to the driver, urging us to stay inside. He didn't give up on his scenario, the possibility that the smuggler's accomplices were hiding, ready to kill us in these remote rainforests.

Horrific scenes played out in my mind—imagined killers lurking in the darkness, waiting for us. The others were equally unsure about what to do, but the driver kept pointing insistently, and his earlier smile had faded. Though he still had that open-mouthed grin, with his yellowish teeth, it was far from reassuring.

Suddenly, we heard voices—familiar voices—speaking our language. Relief washed over us. Someone else speaking our language gave us the boost we needed, and we quickly jumped out of the van, walking toward the source of the voices. We soon reunited with other groups from the airport, including the young woman, Rema, with her little daughter. I never thought I'd be so happy to see her again, but meeting others meant we were in the right place. It was a huge relief to see so many people there—at least, for now, it wasn't about killing us. Moreover, having families around us felt comforting, a sign of safety in this otherwise terrifying night. Still, there was no sign of Meherdad.

Perhaps they could sense the worry on my face, as a boy approached me without me saying a word. He said, "Auntie, Meherdad is walking behind us. He's with us, but a few minutes behind. We can't stop; we need to keep moving. Don't worry." I wanted to wait for him to catch up, but the boy insisted I shouldn't break the line—that it was better to continue moving. He reassured me that I would meet Meherdad at "STOP", the name given by the smuggler for the place where we would board the boat. According to him, we had to reach a STOP sign as soon as possible, since the boat wouldn't wait for anyone.

We knew we needed to walk through the forest to get to STOP, then traverse some distance through water to board the boat, but everyone seemed to be talking about STOP as we walked in line, and there was a nervous energy. The only topic was how far we needed to walk in the forest to reach this STOP, and how much longer it would take. With no sign of life or light, we moved forward, our fear of being caught by the police weighing heavily on us.

The reason the smuggler had chosen to start our journey in the dead of night was also clear—there was a high chance of us being caught. We had heard that the police often knew the routes smugglers used, and that even if we made it to STOP, there was a chance they would be waiting there. The stories about Indonesian jails were terrible, and the only way to avoid that fate was to bribe the police—and no one knew how much would be enough.

A young, beautiful woman with a nearly 14-year-old son walked in front of me. From her words, I gathered that her husband was also with us, though I couldn't see him around. She spoke calmly to her son, behaving in a way that seemed reasonable and reassuring to me—a sign that she came from a "normal" family, or at least a family that was stable. I hardly spoke to her, but it warmed my heart to have someone like her near me. I couldn't help worrying about Meherdad, though. Where was he? The young men who passed by kept assuring me that he was walking behind them, but the longer we walked, the less I believed them. How big was this line, and why couldn't I see him?

Their reassurances, instead of calming me, only heightened my worry. It seemed that everyone knew him well; he had spent a lot of time with the young men around the pool. Amidst my constant worrying, I felt as if I were in a surreal movie—nothing about this situation felt real. The events of that night were like scenes from an action movie, rather than anything resembling real life.

Where is this STOP? It felt like hours had passed, and still, there was no sign of this elusive "STOP" that we were supposed to reach. Although we lacked torches, the brightness of the full moon overhead provided just enough illumination to discern a few steps ahead and the immediate surroundings. On any normal night, I would have admired the beauty of the moonlight, but tonight, it was more of a lifeline to all of us. I don't think anyone here cared about its beauty; we were just thankful for its light.

Now I understood why they chose nights with a full moon—when the sky was illuminated enough to guide our steps. But if the smugglers knew to choose nights with full moons for this reason, surely the Indonesian police did too. Perhaps those who worried about the police waiting for us at STOP were right. I was no longer just vaguely worried about some disaster; now, I had a very specific reason to be more afraid.

A very young boy, aged between 12 and 14, walked next to me. He had a super cheerful attitude, seeming entirely unaffected by fear or worry. His name was Mahdi, and surprisingly, at his age, he was traveling all by himself. From what I could gather, Mahdi had already attempted this journey once before. He told me they had set sail, but the boat had broken down after a few hours, and they all had to come back to wait for another turn. I had heard about what happened to their group when we were at the motel—everyone had been talking about them. Mahdi mentioned that the smugglers always used different places and called them STOPs, and although it was dark, he assured us this was not the same path they had walked previously.

We were all tired, but we had no choice—we needed to keep walking until we reached the shore. From there, we would need to wade through the water for about 15 minutes before we could board, since the boats couldn't come too close to the shore. I had heard this part of the plan before, even back when I was still at home. At least for this, I was prepared—I had bought proper shoes that could be tightly fastened and wouldn't fall off when I waded through the water. Otherwise, I'd be walking barefoot over the sharp stones and sand at the ocean's bottom, something I certainly wanted to avoid.

As Mahdi continued talking, I learned that others among us—including the young, beautiful woman named Tara, who was walking nearby with her teenage son, Hamid—had also been with him during his previous boarding experience. Mahdi kept reassuring me, walking alongside me with a cheerful face and a big smile. He spoke to others too, but I seemed to be his main listener. It struck me that no one else seemed to take him seriously, which I couldn't understand, as he was such a nice and friendly boy.

He was a simple and naive companion, constantly engaging me in conversation about various topics, mostly focusing on his previous experience of attempting the journey. It was a very interesting topic for me, and listening to him turned out to be the best medicine I could have hoped for—it helped pass the time and keep the stress at bay. In hindsight, his presence during those moments felt like a blessing. He warmed my heart far more than I could warm his, especially as he eagerly called me "Auntie" and spoke to me with such familiarity. It was clear that he missed his parents desperately, just as I missed my own son.

Others in our group continued walking and discussing our destination, STOP, in hushed voices. They seemed careful not to attract unnecessary attention. Suddenly, someone exclaimed a little louder, "There it is—the STOP! I can see it!" Excitement grew among the group as we approached the shore. People quickened their pace toward STOP, where the main boat had landed. Similarly, Mahdi and I hurried our steps. We were getting closer, but there was still no sign of Meherdad. It must have been a very long line of people walking—much longer than I had imagined.

As more and more people saw a sign of approaching STOP, their pace increased. You could feel the tension in the air ease slightly, as everyone felt at least some relief at getting closer to our destination.

For me, it was a bit different. Walking faster was impossible. I had a bad history with my left foot, which forced me to take each step carefully. The darkness only made it harder, as I couldn't see where I was placing my feet. My slow pace resulted in me falling into a hole—my left foot got stuck while my right foot remained above ground. Everyone else was running towards STOP, but I was left there, trapped. I couldn't see how deep the hole was; all I knew was that I couldn't pull my foot out. It wasn't large enough for me to twist my foot to free it.

Everyone was already moving quickly ahead of me. I simply couldn't match their speed. Time was against us—we had to reach the boat quickly, and the boat had to depart before dawn. There was always the terrifying possibility that the Indonesian police could find us once the darkness was gone. The darker it was, the safer we were. Being caught meant imprisonment or worse. For many of us, and definitely for me, being imprisoned or blackmailed was not something I could handle.

Some passengers, like Mahdi, had been waiting for this night for a long time—they had spent everything they had in Indonesia just to wait for this opportunity. Many were now so poor they couldn't even afford food. I had heard that in such cases, the smugglers provided them just enough food to survive, but if anyone dared to argue or question the smugglers, they were left on their own, with no choice but to return home. For many, this was the worst possible outcome—worse than drowning in the ocean. How could anyone face what was waiting for them in Iran and their family empty-handed, after spending all their money?

I shouted for help, loudly and desperately, but everyone was too focused on reaching the boat. Now that the boat could be seen at STOP, the urgency had grown. People moved loudly through the sand and stones, the boat only about two kilometers away—or maybe even farther. A smaller boat would take us to the larger one that would carry us on our journey, but the key was to get onto that smaller boat first. To do that, we would have to wade through water up to our shoulders, or at least for me—being a short person. While others advanced, I stayed trapped with my foot in that hole, trying again and again to free myself. My cries were lost in the chaos, drowned out by the shouts and screams of others afraid of being left behind.

Nobody would stop to help, no matter the reason for vulnerability—old age, illness, or injury. In moments like this, people revealed their true selves. Although I was terrified, I could understand why nobody would risk wasting their precious time for me.

I had been trapped for about ten minutes, shouting and pleading, seeing the others running toward the water. I thought for sure that they would leave me behind, that I would be stuck there forever. Suddenly, I saw Mahdi's face, filled with fear, as he ran towards me. He tried to pull me out. I raised my hand to him, and the warmth of his hand reached my heart at that moment. After several attempts, his young strength succeeded where mine had failed, and he pulled me out of that hole. Oh God, I couldn't believe it— You had sent this young angel to save me.

I was finally free, but my body ached all over, especially my injured foot. There was no time to dwell on the pain; I had to keep moving, even with an aching body. We waded into the water, Mahdi holding my hand. He moved ahead of me a little, and it seemed like we were falling even further behind the others. No one cared about what had happened to me—not even myself. Simply surviving that hole, which I had thought would be my tomb, was enough to make me feel blessed.

This little angel, Mahdi, ever positive, gave me instructions on how to walk in the water—how to put my feet firmly on the sand and rocks. He held my hand kindly, as I was even slower now due to my injured foot. But thanks to my shoes, which stayed on even when I was stuck, I didn't have to worry about sharp stones or objects cutting my injured foot further. I could never thank this young boy enough—he was more of a man than anyone else that night.

Among the eighty people walking in that line of uncertainty, only Mahdi was my hero. It seems that the younger you are, the more selfless you act. From that night onward, this angel became my friend, and despite losing contact for some time later due to what happened to him, our friendship remained a lasting and treasured part of my life.

They say you never meet a person by chance. I met Mahdi, Meherdad, and so many others during this journey under the worst circumstances imaginable. Some of them are gone now—moved on to another place. Some I have lost contact with completely, not knowing where they are or what they are doing. But Mahdi, with his heroism that night, left an indelible mark on my heart. Whether they did good or bad, those who joined me on this journey revealed their true selves—there was no time to hide behind trauma or burdens.

After wading through the water, we needed to board a smaller boat, which would take us some distance to the main boat. These smaller boats were really tiny—at most, they could hold five people—but each time, there were no less than fifteen people crammed in. It wasn't uncommon for these boats to turn over due to the high number of passengers they carried.

I heard that the man at the front of the line, the one who had first seen the STOP sign, was also the first to board the smaller boat. One after another, people got in, each time waiting impatiently for their turn, as the boat couldn't carry too many at once. Despite the chaos, we were lucky that there were three smaller boats available to ferry us to the larger one.

Compared to the small boat, the main boat might be called "big," though that was only relative; it wasn't a large boat by any standard. Anyway, one of the "Twelve Labors" for us was just catching the smaller boat. There was no priority for women or children as you might see in movies—all you could hear were people screaming and pushing each other to get on board first.

Finally, I was fortunate enough to get onto the small boat, thanks once again to Mahdi, who pushed me ahead of himself. He assured me he would join us soon, pointing to my injured foot as a reason for his gesture. As we got closer to the larger boat, I got a better look at it—it was just a small fishing boat, slightly bigger than the one we were in now. It wasn't close enough to swim to, even if one were a good swimmer. We were all too exhausted from the forest walk; even the younger men seemed incapable of swimming that distance, and for me, it was out of the question with my injured foot. I was sure my ankle was broken.

From what I could see, the larger boat was barely fit to carry fifteen or twenty people—truth be told, I doubted it was designed for even that number. Yet it had to accommodate far more than that, and none of us were willing to be left behind. We all knew the boat wasn't suitable—either by technical standards or capacity—but no one wanted to be the one to stay.

Everyone around me was impatient, eager to get on board. Some of the women were crying, trying to calm down their children, who were equally terrified. A small boy, maybe around four years old, caught my attention. His mother clung to him tightly, but she was also crying loudly, cursing her husband for putting them in this situation: "I didn't want to travel this way—you forced us!" The poor child was silent, staring at his mother with wide, terrified eyes. It was heartbreaking, but I felt frozen—unable to act or react—merely a witness to this heartbreaking scene.

I think I was the only woman there who wasn't screaming or crying. The little boy looked at me, his gaze filled with surprise. His mother was in enough of a state, and perhaps he felt it was his duty to stay quiet and composed. In a small, timid voice, he asked me, "Auntie, why aren't you crying? Aren't you scared?" I will never forget that innocent look in his eyes. I reached out and gently patted his hair. Somehow, that small gesture seemed to comfort him, much like Mahdi's presence comforted me. I whispered, "Don't be scared, my love; this is just a game for adults to play."

The boat was packed, and I could hardly see anything. I turned and caught sight of Mahdi, standing next to me, with no trace of fear on his face, just his usual smile—teasing others for their fears. I felt a pang of sorrow for him. Was he really not afraid, or was he hiding it even from himself? He knew too much for a boy his age—barely fourteen. He had no choice but to grow up too fast. It was as if I had become a substitute for Mahdi's absent mother, and in return, he saw me as a mother figure too. At that moment, we both drew strength from each other. It is remarkable how, in times of need and despair, a stranger can become the closest person to you.

The little boy continued holding onto his mother, but after our brief exchange, he gave me a smile—the most beautiful smile I had ever seen. It was a smile of comfort, of reassurance. For him, the most frightening part was not the scene we were in, but his mother's fear. Seeing his smile gave me something beautiful to focus on, something to cling to amidst the chaos. I realized then that it wasn't me calming the boy, but rather it was his presence—and Mahdi's—that calmed me down.

The youthful spirit in Mahdi and the innocent energy of the little boy were what kept me grounded. They reminded me of the one thing we adults often forget: not to take everything too seriously. Their carefree attitude was like a lifeline. Surprisingly, no one else took Mahdi's light-heartedness seriously, but I personally think it was a kind of survival for all of us. Even in the midst of all this discomfort and fear, he didn't stop being funny, making jokes—even about the boat size and how it swayed with the load of people, as if it would tip over any minute. We all gripped tightly onto some part of the boat, holding on as if our lives depended on it—which they did. I could feel the pressure in my hand, the tightness in my grip, born from fear.

The little boy's innocence brought my thoughts back to my own children. It struck me how often memories of my kids were triggered when I saw other children. For the first time in my life, I was grateful they weren't there with me. It was a relief not to have my kids around at that moment, as I would probably have been just like that screaming mother. It was easier when I only had to worry about my own life—I could face danger for myself, but not for my children. Everyone here was responsible for themselves and their families. For my own life, I could make sacrifices, but risking my children's lives—that was something I wasn't brave enough to do.

Perhaps the people here were so desperate for a new life that they were willing to take any risk, no matter what it entailed. Today was not the day for judgment. It might have felt like the end of the world, but when you are begging for your life, there is no time or energy for judgment—you just need a chance to survive, at any cost.

Taking your life in a small bag and trying to spread it somewhere else—that isn't a crime. Even if, by some chance, you are a sinner, there is always a way to redeem yourself. I wasn't justifying crime; I knew that wrongdoing should be met with consequences. But today, here, we weren't criminals. We were just human beings who wanted to live a few more days, experience some freedom, or maybe a happily-ever-after in what we called a "promised land." Whether or not such a place existed, we had an obligation to our dignity to at least try to reach it.

Amidst all this chaos and ugliness, there was a kind of beauty in not being judged. Reality was raw, laid bare—like an award-winning movie with no heroes. None of us wanted to be the hero of that scene; all we wanted was to stay alive. Was that too much to ask?

These sharp ideas fought in my tired head, perhaps because I was trying to distract myself from the pain in my damaged foot. Mahdi was still beside me, holding my arm, carrying my tired body. His mature behavior was proof that I was right. This very young boy was more of a man than many of the adults there.

Chapter Nine

We finally made it close to the larger boat, but now another challenge awaited me—we had to somehow climb from the small boat to the main one. How could I possibly manage this with my injured foot? Being short and not particularly strong only added to the difficulty, making the task seem almost insurmountable. Even while wading in the water, my height had made things harder. The water reached up to my chest, while others found it more manageable.

Mahdi was trying his best to convince me that it wasn't as hard as it looked. Since he had encountered a similar situation just a month ago, his familiarity with the process seemed to give him confidence. Their boat had broken down after 24 hours, forcing them into a difficult return journey. Yet somehow, Mahdi managed to recount these hardships in a lighthearted way, treating them as a humorous tale of misfortune.

I saw a young girl, probably in her late twenties, named Mina. She was holding the hand of another older woman—Selma, her mother. Mina's face was filled with fear, tears streaming down as she yelled, calling her mother by name. Perhaps calling her mother's name aloud gave her a sense of comfort, like all of us who instinctively think of our mothers in the most challenging moments. Selma held her daughter's hand tightly but remained silent, as if trying to absorb her daughter's fear. Mina turned her face towards me, and in a broken voice said, "Can you see what a disaster we willingly brought into our lives?"

Another boy, whom I had never met before—even back at the motel—was shouting loudly, calling out, "Mother, don't be afraid! I am here with you." It struck me that he was shouting these words not for anyone else, but for himself—words that he desperately needed to hear. He needed a mother to say, "Don't be afraid, I am here," but since no one could fill that role, he shouted it for himself. A few hours ago, when I had been begging for someone to help me out of the hole, they all could hear me, but no one except Mahdi truly responded.

Mahdi was laughing at them, and I wasn't sure if it was out of fear or a kind of amazement at the absurdity of it all. I strained to look up at the main boat, which was still some distance away. It wasn't much larger than the small boat that had brought us here. Though it was larger, it still seemed grossly inadequate to accommodate a crowd of nearly one hundred people, not to mention the children we had with us. How could this boat possibly be reliable?

Mahdi, Mina, and others who had experienced the sailing process before insisted that this boat was better than the previous ones they'd been on. They spoke of the other boats they had boarded and described them as being in much worse condition. But even with Mahdi's attempt to reassure me, I couldn't help but wonder, "How do you know if this one won't have technical problems too?"

Mina, her mother, and that boy—everyone was fighting their own fears in their own way. Some were vocal, crying out, while others like Selma were silent, taking the burden inward. Mahdi's laughter, Mina's tears, and the boy's loud proclamations—all of these emotions mingled in the air, capturing the depth of our collective fear, hope, and desperate need to survive.

We had made it to the next stage, but each step only revealed a new challenge. We were trapped between our fears, our desperation, and the hope for a better future. Even standing on that fragile boat, with the uncertainty of what awaited us, we somehow found the courage to keep moving forward, buoyed by each other's presence. Mahdi's laughter, Mina's fear, the boy's desperate calls—these were the voices that echoed through the night, pushing us forward towards whatever lay ahead.

My short height, injured foot, and lack of athleticism made climbing onto the bigger boat seem nearly impossible. I pushed with my hands, trying multiple times to pull myself up, but each attempt ended in failure. The people waiting behind me grew visibly impatient, with murmurs of frustration reaching my ears. Just as I was on the verge of giving up, a big hand suddenly pushed me up from behind, and I finally managed to board the boat. I couldn't see which of the young men had helped me; all I could think in that moment was, "Oh, I am up, finally." The realization that a stranger had touched my body in such a way brought a bit of embarrassment, but I quickly shrugged it off. He had probably grown tired of waiting for me to keep failing, and in that moment, we had to let go of such social standards—survival was all that mattered.

Water dripped from my body and soaked my clothes. I wasn't alone—everyone else was soaked through, too—cold, tired, hungry, and desperate for even a few moments of rest. As soon as I got onto the boat, I sought out a corner, a place where I could lean my back, trying to overcome the exhaustion that had taken over. I needed to check on my damaged foot, but the surface of the boat was as hard as bedrock. Comfort was out of the question—just finding a place to sit down was a small victory, given how many of us were crammed into the boat. The space was so tight that moving was almost impossible, but at least I could sit.

Leaning against the side of the boat for a few minutes gave me a chance to regain some clarity. Gradually, I began to see those around me more clearly. Mahdi was nowhere to be seen, but I noticed Mohammad and Zara, the young couple we had shared a room with back at the motel. They sat in front of me, and there were a few others scattered around them. Next to me was a handsome young man with an athletic build named Faraz. Unlike everyone else, he didn't call me Auntie; instead, he politely asked for my surname and addressed me with it from then on. We exchanged only a few words.

It had never happened to me before, even in all those commercial trips I had taken in the past—no one sitting next to me on a plane had ever asked for my surname. Faraz introduced himself as a professional athlete, and I couldn't help but think, "Perhaps he could be helpful in an emergency." But the memory of being left behind in that hole earlier crossed my mind. Everyone had heard my cries for help, yet no one came except Mahdi. How could I expect anyone to help now? I quickly shook off the thought. "Let's hope for the best," I told myself. No use dwelling on negative possibilities now.

We were all here now, almost everyone had made it onto the boat. This journey would be the same for all of us, whether we wanted it or not. I was so tired that I almost forgot to think about Meherdad—where was he? Even if he had been at the end of the line, he should have made it by now. I turned to one of the boys, someone who seemed to know Meherdad. He came closer and, with a calm and gentle voice, sympathy clear in his eyes, said, "Meherdad and his group got lost at the airport. They ended up taking the wrong flight, and he had to go back to Jakarta. He's safe there, but he won't be joining us on this trip."

My heart pounded so loudly I was sure everyone could hear it. My jaw dropped as I struggled to comprehend what he was saying. What would happen now? I had promised his father that we would be together throughout this journey. Meherdad's carefree attitude—always wandering off—had finally caught up with him. Seeing my distress, the boy reassured me, "He's okay. He just missed joining the group on time. They will send him out on the next turn—maybe just a day behind us. You will definitely see each other in Australia. Just pray that everything goes well for all of us, and we all make it to our destination."

I couldn't hold back my tears, but I tried not to create a scene. Everyone, including myself, was far too exhausted for any emotional drama. I kept quiet, silently letting the tears fall. If Meherdad was safe in Jakarta, then perhaps he was better off than I was—for now, at least. I tried to take comfort in that thought.

I was overwhelmed by tiredness, and falling asleep from exhaustion was inevitable. But it wasn't a restful sleep; it was more like passing out from sheer fatigue. When I woke up, people around me were still unsettled, some walking around the boat, despite everyone being onboard. I felt pain in my foot, especially my knee, but it wasn't unbearable. This was a good sign—thankfully, it seemed nothing was broken.

The boat still hadn't set sail, further proof that my sleep had been more of a blackout rather than a restful sleep. I thought to myself, "Where I found to sit is good enough," as long as I could lean my back on something to support my exhausted body.

Soon, I heard the engine starting, signaling our departure. It saddened me deeply that Meherdad wasn't here. Perhaps it was fate that we were separated. The few who sat close to the engine cabin, including me, had been kind enough earlier to keep reassuring me that Meherdad was behind us in the line. They clearly wanted to spare me from worry. Now, as the boat began to move, I could feel something inside me shatter. My travel companion, my beloved nephew, was somewhere else, and there was a real possibility that I might never see him again. I prayed silently that he would get another chance to board safely when his turn came.

But deep down, I couldn't help feeling consumed by sadness—would I ever be able to see him again? What if they weren't telling me the truth? Some speculated that he and the others with him might have been detained by Indonesian police, leading to a potential nightmare in jail. If that were true, what could I do? I felt utterly helpless, incapable of assisting him in any way. In this way of migration, expecting help from others is foolish—especially given the situation we were trapped in.

The young, beautiful, and talkative mother Rema, whom I had met at the motel, sat beside me with her little girl, Aram. She was constantly chatting with the young boys around her, and it seemed she was quite popular. The boys hovered around her, though one appeared to be closer to her than the rest. At first, I thought this one might be her husband, someone I hadn't seen before. He seemed attentive, even taking care of the child. However, I soon learned that she was a single mother. She tearfully mentioned that they hadn't eaten in a long time.

I offered her one of the canned food items I had brought in my backpack, and the young man took over the task of feeding the child while Rema resumed her animated conversation with the others. It was as though she was at a family gathering, talking to relatives she hadn't seen in years, with no hint of worry about our current circumstances.

In front of us sat the other beautiful woman I had met earlier—Tara, with her teenage son, Hamid. This time, her husband was with them. He soon introduced himself as a mechanic and mentioned that he had been with Mahdi, Selma, and Mina during their failed boarding attempt previously. It was a bit of a comfort to have a mechanic among us in case of any problems with the boat, but he had been there in the other failed attempt as well, and they hadn't made it. It reminded me how worn out these boats truly were.

He explained to others how much he had tried to fix the boat the last time, but despite his efforts, it had been in such poor condition that there was no saving it. Even with all his skills, he couldn't work miracles on a boat that simply wasn't built to survive. I asked him what he thought about this boat, and he replied, "I can't say yet, but I am scared." When I asked why, he said, "Because if I just go and take a look, and by chance, it's as bad as the last one, everyone will blame me if something goes wrong. It's exactly what happened last time."

He continued, "People forget that smugglers always choose the most worn-out boats, since they never intend for these boats to return. Why would they spend a huge amount of money on a reliable boat if it's only a one-way trip? But there are almost a hundred people here, including children. There's a big chance we could be lost at sea. Even with the best boats, it's a risky journey, and with these ones, our chances of survival might be only 10 to 20 percent. Maybe the smugglers think that's enough—if we're willing to risk everything, then they make it a real risk."

Tara listened silently. She looked terrified, and it was clear that she wasn't doing well. She was already getting seasick, and the boat hadn't even truly started moving yet.

Meherdad remained on my mind throughout the journey, and I resolved to maintain a positive outlook. Perhaps he had returned to our previous hotel and was safe. Being young and strong, he possessed an advantage in a situation as unusual as ours. Youth and strength were essential qualities for evading trouble during such an unpredictable journey.

After all, I understood that unexpected events could occur at any time during any trip, and this journey was no exception—in fact, surprises should be expected even more here. However, I had no control over what came to my mind—bad, good, or worst, and I had mentally prepared myself for even worse scenarios than simply getting lost at the airport—a possibility that could befall anyone without the ability to communicate verbally. Still, I couldn't shake off my concern for Meherdad, not even for a moment. I held onto hope that he was alright.

I shouted internally to myself: "Stop! Think about yourself like everyone else does, OK?"

Hours passed as the boat navigated through the ocean, with none of us having any idea of our location. The boat staff consisted of three men—two young and one older, who seemed to be the semi-captain. One of them looked experienced, like he knew what he was doing, while we had no choice but to trust this middle-aged, seemingly unskilled Indonesian man operating the boat. He had two younger assistants, neither of whom could utter a single word about the engine, and the worst part was that none of us could communicate with them.

The boat was making its way through the ocean, and the suffocating smell of gasoline overwhelmed us. Despite this, I thought to myself: "Where I am sitting now is the safest place on this boat." Most of those around me were families, while the other part of the boat was filled with single young men, some of whom had very strange, almost criminal looks—or at least, that was what my weak nerves made me think. Probably it was my constant fear and insecurity creating such impressions. I refused to move to another seat; even with the gasoline fumes, I felt somehow safer here.

Suddenly, one of the young boys, who had been below deck with a few other men near the engine, jumped up and exclaimed that the engine had malfunctioned and would soon stop. Panic spread quickly among the passengers. Fortunately, Tara's husband, Ahmed, the mechanic, was close by. He went below deck to the engine room, and after about twenty minutes, we heard the engine roaring to life again.

Joyful exclamations resounded throughout the boat. However, the relief was short-lived as the engine ceased functioning once more. Ahmed, the mechanic, and others worked tirelessly for a few hours. Each time, the engine would start for nearly fifteen minutes before stopping again. They tried many more times, but no progress was made. The Indonesian captain joined us and, through gestures, conveyed that it was useless—the engine would not keep running, and even if it did, it might stop again after a few hours, and by then, we could be too far out in the ocean to reach any place safe.

He told us with sign language that we needed to abandon the boat soon, but how? We were some distance away from the shore—should we swim in the middle of the ocean? He somehow made us understand that we were not so far from shore that we couldn't get to solid ground, though it wouldn't be the same place we started from. He steered the boat closer to the shore, explaining—again in sign language—that we could walk along the shoreline rather than risk drowning with the boat, and like in any similar situation, we had no choice but to trust him.

Once again, the same scene played out as we disembarked the boat. Everyone scrambled to get off, with no regard for anyone else. Then, I saw Mahdi among the other singles, and

God knows how happy I was that he appeared once more—like an angel. Again, this young boy displayed more maturity than any of the supposedly strong men with their imposing physiques. He took my hand and helped me off the boat.

    I was hesitant to step onto the unknown ground, but Mahdi, with his gentle voice, spoke to me as if I were a child—reassuring, telling me nothing was going to happen, that it wasn't as deep as I imagined. I trusted this young man completely; he had already proven himself to be reliable.

Chapter Ten

We dragged our tired, wet bodies through the stones and sand once again, taking slow steps through the water. Finally, we reached the beach, surrounded by darkness and uncertainty. We had no idea where we were, but the sight of many doors around us indicated that we were in a village—not a completely remote area. This was a hopeful sign for desperate people like us in the middle of the night. But now, which door could we knock on for help?

After a few minutes, someone informed us that the Indonesian crew—the captain and his two assistants—had fled. How they managed to leave if the boat was broken, we never found out. All we knew was that we were nearly a hundred strangers, stranded in the middle of nowhere, with no means of verbal communication and no idea where we were. The ugly reality of our journey, which had previously been just negative thoughts and frightening possibilities, was now staring us in the face.

We spotted a few houses belonging to the nearby villagers. Some individuals knocked on their doors, seeking assistance, while another called the smuggler to explain our situation. The smuggler managed to speak with the villagers over the phone, instructing them on how to help us. Soon, a local villager allowed us to take shelter in his garden. Strangely, the villagers who came to guide us into their large garden showed no surprise at seeing nearly a hundred people at their doorstep in the middle of the night. It was clear that this wasn't an unusual occurrence for them, which only deepened the strangeness of our experience.

Desperate and exhausted, we settled into the garden, waiting for whatever came next. I tried to make sense of the situation—how these villagers could remain so calm about a hundred strangers knocking on their door in the dead of night. This seemed to be a situation they had faced many times before.

While we waited, everyone around me began spinning their own wild and disheartening scenarios. People were whispering fears and creating stories based on their imagination—each scenario more ominous than the last. Amidst the chaos, I chose to listen only to Mahdi. He had recounted his previous experience of a similar failed journey—how the boat had broken down, and eventually, help had arrived. His words carried a glimmer of hope, and in that moment, that hope was all I had. More fear and stress were the last things I needed right now.

The place we were calling our temporary refuge wasn't particularly large, but it was big enough for us to scatter in small groups of five or six. The garden didn't have many plants; it was mostly covered with compacted soil. The owner, who we later learned was a farmer, had already spoken with the smuggler, so he knew what was happening. He ran around, seemingly unfazed and surprisingly friendly, offering whatever limited assistance he could.

Some of the people began sharing whatever food they had brought in their bags, while others, in typical fashion, started giving lectures about what they thought was going to happen next.

While some other passengers calmly played cards, acting as though nothing unusual had happened, perhaps they were the ones acting wisely. In a journey like ours, one should expect anything—good or bad. Every incident, no matter how drastic, had to be accepted as normal. I chose to sit beside the young couple I had met at the motel, as well as the mechanic, Ahmed, and his family. It seemed like Ahmed and his wife had found their match in the young couple and had quickly become friendly. The mechanic and his wife seemed surprisingly young to have a teenage son, and being near them made me feel not only safer but also like I had more in common with them compared to the other individuals. They appeared to be more "normal" to me in a way that was comforting.

Generously, Mohammad—the young man—began sharing his canned food with others. It wasn't common in such circumstances for people to share; usually, everyone saved whatever they had for other potential incidents. But Mohammad opened his bag and gave away most of his canned food to others. This one small act proved to me that I had chosen the right people to trust. He distributed the food among groups with a big smile, despite the limited supply. Luckily, I had some water and biscuits in my bag, which I shared with Rema and her child, Aram. Even though I didn't particularly like Rema, I couldn't turn a blind eye to her hungry child. Surprisingly, Rema never seemed ready to take responsibility for her daughter, always relying on others.

Finally, I spotted Mahdi among the group. He was chatting away, sharing his previous experience about the boat breakdown, as usual. My foot was still in considerable pain, but it wasn't unbearable. I waved to Mahdi to come over and gave him some of my food. It was amazing to see that he still wouldn't stop smiling, not for a second. He finished the food in the blink of an eye, and I thought to myself, wherever Meherdad was, he was probably in better condition than us.

After some time, a few of the men, including Ahmed, the mechanic, decided to go to the nearest city to find a vehicle large enough to transport us all. The smuggler had given them instructions on what to do. They left for a few hours, and this unexpected gathering seemed to turn into a kind of happy party in their absence. As we found out, the nearest residence was about 15 minutes away, so there was no risk in making as much noise as they wanted—and they certainly did.

Before sunrise, the farmer returned with Ahmed and two other men. Ahmed seemed like a reasonable person. While he was away, a nonsensical rumor spread among the passengers that he was the one responsible for breaking the boat's engine, the same way some accused him during their previous failed journey. I remembered him predicting that such accusations might arise. Poor man—how easily people could be ungrateful.

Mahdi was sharing his opinions non-stop, just like always, though it seemed nobody took him seriously due to his age. Yet his confidence never wavered, and he didn't seem to care about the dismissive attitudes of others. Ahmed's son, Hamid, was a few years older than Mahdi but was the complete opposite—quiet, always following his parents closely. Whether it was due to their strict upbringing or respect for his parents, Hamid remained reserved. Whatever the reason, Ahmed provided his family with great support—something I had never experienced from anyone in my own life.

Ahmed and the others informed us that they had managed to hire a large truck from the city to transport us to a different location—a place with slightly better access to facilities, though still not exactly the city. The smuggler had arranged for buses to meet us there and take us to a hotel. Although we didn't know exactly where we were heading, the smuggler had given Ahmed an address. At least we hadn't been abandoned completely, which gave us all a glimmer of hope.

We pooled some money to pay the farmer for his kindness. As we queued up to board the truck, we said goodbye to the farmer and his family, who waved at us with huge smiles on their faces. It felt strange—a mixture of gratitude and uncertainty—as we embarked on yet another leg of our journey, hoping that, this time, we would finally make it to safety.

It was a big truck, but not nearly big enough to transport a hundred people. From what others said, I learned it was usually used for transporting animals, and the smell of animal waste made that clear. We boarded the truck one by one—no priority was given to women or children, just like the scramble to board the boat. Everyone was simply trying to survive.

Since there wasn't enough space, we had to stand, packed tightly against each other. It was an incredibly uncomfortable moment, being pressed so close to men I didn't know. I tried my best to stand as firmly as possible, hoping no one would touch me, but it was impossible. As the truck moved through unfamiliar roads, we were in darkness, which added to our stress and uncertainty.

By the time we reached a large roundabout, it was almost twilight. There were some shops around the area, and the smuggler had advised us to scatter so as not to draw too much attention. But with so many people, all of whom looked so different from the locals, we were bound to attract attention anyway. The smuggler provided an address for another location where a few buses were supposed to be waiting to take us to a hotel, which had been booked in advance.

I looked around and realized I couldn't see Ahmed and his family or the young couple, Mohammad and Zara. They were not among the others who had disembarked. Later, I found out that when Ahmed had spoken to the smuggler on the phone, he was the first to find out the hotel's address. Before sharing it with anyone else, he took his own family there first to make sure the situation was safe. Only then did he call someone in our group to give them the location of the bus and the hotel where his family was now accommodated.

It was completely out of character, or at least out of the moral compass I thought he had. Some people were furious at him, saying he had betrayed us, while others felt he was taking revenge for being falsely accused of breaking the boat engine. After all the calculations I had made about who I could trust, it turned out I was wrong. I found myself standing all alone in that massive roundabout, feeling more isolated than ever.

Suddenly, I heard Rema's voice calling out to me: "Mommy, come here!" I saw her standing with a few other men, hiring a van to take them to the location where the buses were waiting. She was talking non-stop about Ahmed and his actions, and though her chatter usually annoyed me, she was right this time. It was not how someone should behave, especially after everything we'd been through together.

Finally, we reached a street where several buses were lined up, waiting for us. Relief washed over everyone, and for a moment, happiness broke through our exhaustion. We were smelly, dirty, and still in our wet clothes, but at least we were finally getting some semblance of comfort.

The moment I sat down on the bus, I felt an overwhelming wave of fatigue. I fell asleep almost instantly, barely aware of my surroundings. I woke up a few times, taking short glances around, and saw that everyone else was asleep as well. No one cared about anything else—we were too drained, too overwhelmed, and just glad to have a seat to rest on. The bus became our brief refuge, a place where, if only for a few hours, we could forget the horrors of the journey and let our exhausted bodies rest.

Finally, the buses stopped in front of a hotel. Maybe it was a two-star hotel, but in such a situation, it felt like pure luxury. We were soon led to our rooms, and, to my dismay, I found out I was sharing a room with Rema and her little daughter, Aram. Oh no, not again. But I reminded myself that she was the one who had helped me get on the bus. Without her, I might still be wandering around that roundabout, confused and exhausted.

Although Rema had been my savior in some sense, I still couldn't bring myself to like her. I was far too worn out to endure her nonstop talking and her loud, intrusive voice. Yet, I had no other choice. She kindly offered, "You take a shower first, and then I'll bathe with my daughter." I thought, Well, that's nice of her. Later, I realized her gesture wasn't entirely altruistic—it was more about getting a chance to rummage through my bag while I was in the shower.

It wasn't exactly a secret that Rema couldn't be trusted. She had proven herself shady on multiple occasions. I knew that if I left my bag with her, she'd be tempted. Thankfully, I had nothing of value in it. Before I embarked on this journey, I had asked a tailor to sew a hidden pocket into both cups of my bra, complete with zippers. Each cup had enough space to hide important items without looking suspiciously deformed. It was a precaution I was now grateful for.

Oh, what a blessing that warm water was—running over my tired body, washing away not just the dirt but also the burden I had carried over the past few days. Despite the trials of this journey, these recent days had been far worse than words could describe. Perhaps things would get even worse next, but I didn't want to spoil the joy of the warm water on my skin with anxious thoughts. My inner Scarlet O'Hara wanted to leave those worries for tomorrow. Right now, I just wanted to enjoy the warmth.

When I stepped out of the shower, I saw I had been right: everything in my bag had been moved around. I knew Rema couldn't be trusted, so I purposely left the water running, pretending I was still showering. Suddenly, I opened the bathroom door, catching her completely off guard, bent over my bag with the zipper still open. She looked up, startled, and immediately shouted, her voice rude and defensive: "Why did you leave the water running? Do you think I'm trying to steal your things?" I just looked at her, smiled, and instead of answering her accusations, said calmly, "There isn't enough shampoo in the bathroom. I'll call reception to bring you some."

She understood the meaning of my smile perfectly. Her face tightened in frustration, but she was too brazen to care. She grabbed her daughter in a rush and stormed off to the bathroom, her voice raised in irritation, mainly because she hadn't found what she was looking for. It was all so normal to her, as if searching someone else's belongings was an everyday occurrence. Why did she think I'd leave anything valuable behind? How foolish.

I picked up the phone and called reception, requesting more shampoo and some bread. I was still smiling, shaking my head at the absurdity of it all. From the bathroom, I could hear Rema's voice echoing—yelling at the poor little girl. Anyone who met her could easily tell what kind of person she was, but it was beyond me how someone could try to steal and then get mad at me for being cautious.

When she finished washing her daughter, she brazenly shouted, "Mommy, can you help dress her so I can finish washing myself?" Unbelievable. By now, nothing about her could surprise me.

I helped little Aram put on her clothes, trying to make her smile while I did. When Rema came out, we ate some of the canned food with bread. She complained loudly, "Why is this food so cold?" I said nothing, ignoring her as best as I could. I really wanted to keep any interaction with her to an absolute minimum.

After we ate, she left the room with her daughter. The moment they were gone, I entrusted my weary body to the clean sheets, sinking into the bed and falling asleep almost instantly.

I didn't realize when Rema returned. By the time I woke up, it was late afternoon, and it had already started getting dark outside. I decided to leave the room as well. The lobby was full of my travel companions, all well-dressed and freshly clean. One of the men informed me that we could eat at the hotel restaurant for free—all expenses were covered by the smuggler.

Delighted, I made my way to the restaurant, where I spotted the two other families—the mechanic with his wife and son, and Mohammad and Zara—sitting at a table, eating and seemingly having a good time. They greeted me warmly, as if nothing unusual had happened. It seemed that in this strange journey of ours, everyone was eager to pretend that nothing had gone wrong.

I didn't ask the mechanic why he had left without notifying the rest of us, taking his family and friends ahead. But, as if sensing my silent disapproval, he immediately began making excuses, even asking the other two couples to back him up. He could tell from my expression that I wasn't buying his excuses. Still, what else could I do? All I knew was that I wouldn't have done the same to them or anyone else. He continued, insisting, "Oh, we couldn't find you," and other feeble explanations. But we all knew the truth—it wouldn't have been hard to find me among the other singles. After all, the number of family groups wasn't that large.

Suddenly, I noticed that some members of the family group weren't there in the hotel. Someone told me that they had hired a taxi and returned directly to Jakarta. Why didn't I think of that? If I had, I could have found Meherdad there as well. Why didn't anyone tell us? If they had, I would have hired a taxi too and gone straight back to Jakarta. It reminded me of being trapped in that hole, left behind by everyone. Perhaps this journey really was like a survival game, one in which you couldn't afford to sacrifice your chance for anyone else.

Throughout this entire journey, and even in situations that lay ahead, I kept encountering moments like this—small betrayals by my travel mates. Each time, it reminded me of why I had left my homeland. I had wanted to escape the mentality of selfishness and survival at any cost. Yet, here I was, faced with the same attitude. It seemed I had no other choice but to go along with it. Is this the beginning of abandoning my values? I wondered. Even if it's just a small issue, it's something I've always despised.

Purposely, I changed the subject, and they were happy to move on. We sat at the table and chatted for a while, while others, with their loud, joyful voices, continued to come into the restaurant. Their voices were so loud that, on a few occasions, a staff member had to warn them, but no one seemed to care.

I ordered a meal and went to the cashier to ask if our orders were being paid for by the smuggler. The cashier made a phone call to someone—I'm not sure who—and then shook his head, denying it. So, I paid for my food and made my way back to my room.

On my way back, I passed some guys sitting in the corridor, chatting. I asked one of them if I could use his phone, and, smiling, he generously handed it to me. I first tried to call Meherdad, but there was no connection. Then, I called my husband, giving him a brief overview of what had happened. I didn't go into too much detail—it was an international call, and I didn't want to take advantage of the man's generosity.

It must have been around eight or nine in the evening when I returned to my room. I washed my dirty clothes—they were as filthy as if I had been through a chimney. The water turned completely black, and I had to wash everything several times. Oh, that means all this dirt had been on my body too. Finally, it was time to get some real rest. I went to bed, and unlike all the other days, falling asleep came to me easily and suddenly.

I really didn't realize when Rema came back. For the first time, she seemed careful not to make any noise that might wake me. It must have been very late, as every time I woke up for a drink or to use the bathroom, she still wasn't there.

Waking up in an actual bed felt like a huge blessing. When I went to the lobby, everyone was talking about how the smuggler had called—we were to head to the airport today to go back to Jakarta. I had a quick breakfast at the café, but then one of the boys called me upstairs to the reception desk. Apparently, the receptionist had issued bills to some of the boys for their food and laundry, and was insisting they pay or he would call the police.

The boys kept arguing, insisting that the smuggler was supposed to cover their expenses. Since I was the only one among them who spoke English, they called me over to help. The receptionist was adamant, threatening to call "the General" if they didn't pay. I asked who this General was, and the others explained that he was a high-ranking, corrupt police officer who worked with the smuggler and took a large cut of the profits. They suspected he was also the one who had arranged our hotel stay, or the receptionist wouldn't have his number.

I thought they might be exaggerating, spinning another one of those elaborate stories that seemed to float around constantly. Yet those who had been in this for longer seemed to have a lot of details about this so-called General. I learned that no one had actually met him or spoken to him directly; even the smuggler communicated with him through intermediaries. This whole mysterious system intrigued me. It fed my curiosity—who could this person be?

When the receptionist finally made the call and handed me the phone, I felt a surge of anticipation. My eyes widened as I took it and asked, "Am I speaking to the General?"

"Yes," he replied.

I explained the situation that the boys had incurred expenses they expected the smuggler to cover, but the receptionist was refusing. He said it was fine and that we should all head to the airport; he would take care of the expenses.

I could feel my voice trembling slightly. Here I was, talking to this enigmatic figure, and it stirred something inside me—a mix of fear and curiosity. I decided to push a bit further, adopting the tone of an insistent customer, which wasn't like me at all.

"How much can you guarantee that we'll reach our destination safely?" I asked.

His response was swift, "I guarantee you'll land in Australia safely." I could sense his mocking smile, even through the phone. You fool, I thought. You're asking for a guarantee on what's essentially a suicide mission?

Then he asked my name. I hesitated—I didn't want to reveal it, but there was no use pretending. Everyone here knew I was the only woman fluent in English. When I stayed silent, he said, "Don't be afraid. I'll inform the smuggler to look out for you. You sound like a courageous and respectable woman from our conversation."

What a jerk, I thought. How could you possibly judge my character from just a few questions?

Do you really think I trusted a man who betrayed his country and was corrupt to his core? Of course not. But I just thanked him and hung up.

As soon as I did, I noticed everyone else was just as curious about him as I was. I learned that not even the smuggler had ever met him, which wasn't surprising—trust didn't come easily in this line of work. I knew from my time as a business interpreter that even in legitimate fields, people often trusted no one.

They said the General always initiated contact from an unknown number, with a middleman who handled all the money and logistics between him and the smuggler. None of the men working for the smuggler ever gave a straight answer, but later, one let it slip they had been in this business for years. They had powerful connections in high-ranking police and security circles. Corruption, it seemed, was everywhere. This time, however, it worked in my favor, and although I didn't like it, I decided to turn a blind eye like everyone else.

His fluent English proved he was educated, someone in a higher position. It confirmed what I had always believed: the big criminals never face consequences, they only rise higher.

When I hung up, I told the others that the General had agreed to pay the boys' expenses, but I kept my question about guarantees to myself.

Despite everything happening, my mind remained on Meherdad. I was especially worried when I tried to call, and he didn't pick up. They told me that his group had taken the wrong flight and returned to Jakarta, back to the motel. One of them claimed to have spoken with him last night, saying he was having a great time. But something felt off. I found myself trusting the smuggler more than these people, and that's saying a lot.

My suspicions grew when the same guy added that Meherdad had been drunk during their conversation. That had to be a lie—Meherdad never drank or smoked, a commitment he always maintained. It fit his athletic discipline. So why were they lying? Was something wrong, and they were just trying to shield me from it?

We needed to head to the airport, but surprisingly, some people didn't even have enough money for a taxi. The cabs were called in shifts, with each group of four heading out separately.

We were told the smuggler would cover the cost of the taxi. It wasn't the money I cared about—it wasn't an amount I couldn't afford—but rather what it symbolized. These little gestures were signs of hope, proof that he wouldn't just abandon us as a scammer. A scammer, yes, but one playing a different kind of game.

Rema, as usual, was in my taxi along with two other boys, all of them spinning their negative scenarios. I asked politely if they could stop, but they ignored me. One even went further, saying, "When this smuggler leaves you behind, just come back to Iran. I'll give you the number of another trustworthy smuggler. He lives in my neighborhood." I stayed silent, hoping my quietness would make them stop, but they couldn't care less.

While we were in the taxi, one of them got a call, then handed me the phone, saying it was Meherdad. I took it with trembling hands, only to hear a young man—but it definitely wasn't Meherdad. He was pretending to be my nephew, talking too familiarly. I cut him off, saying, "You're not Meherdad. What happened to him?" He admitted it wasn't him and claimed Meherdad had just gone shopping. Then he hung up.

Their behavior only made me more suspicious. Something was wrong, and they were trying to shield me, but even a child could see through their clumsy attempts. However, I knew I had to stay calm and play along—it was likely they were just trying to be kind and not worry me. But where was he now? Was he lost, or had he been arrested by the Indonesian police? I knew I could probably handle myself if we faced the authorities, but I doubted Meherdad could. Whatever the truth, I had no control over it. Silence and hope seemed to be my only options for now, even if it was difficult amidst these reckless people.

At the airport, the other groups arrived one after another. We were supposed to stay scattered, but no one really bothered, especially once we found out we were on different flights again, and there would be hours of waiting.

This time, we also learned that although the flight fee had been paid, we still had to cover some additional expenses at the ticket counter. Some people were entirely unprepared. They called the smuggler, but he refused to cover these costs. They kept talking, whispering now, and Rema wandered the airport with her daughter before coming to sit beside me.

With her usual entitlement, she asked, "Mommy, are you going to pay for us?" I couldn't help it; my patience snapped. I replied loudly, "Yes, if I could remember when I gave birth to you today!" She was stunned, her face full of surprise, and thankfully, she walked away silently towards the group of boys, no doubt hunting for someone else to exploit.

After a while, one of the boys approached me, angry. He got close and said, "We decided those with money must pay for others too." He spoke without any hint of politeness, continuing, "We think you have enough, so you should pay for at least three others. Do you have money?" He pointed his finger at me, his tone demanding. It was clear they thought they could intimidate me into compliance.

I raised my voice so others could hear, making it clear I wasn't scared. "Whether I have money or not isn't your concern. I am only paying for myself—not for you, not for anyone else. And if you keep pressing me, I'll go straight to the police. Let's see who they believe—a tourist or someone without any money."

They say the best defense is a strong offense, and it worked. They fell silent, sneaking glances at me for the rest of the time. I decided to stay far away from them until boarding. Even on the plane, I saw them but was glad to see they kept their distance—exactly what I wanted.

The flight wasn't long, but it was late at night when we arrived in Jakarta. The smuggler was still in contact with some of the group and instructed us to take a taxi, then pass the phone to the driver so he could provide the destination. As expected, Rema was in my taxi again, along with two other boys, behaving as if nothing had happened. I kept quiet, knowing that even one word would give them the opportunity to start their nonsense again. Exhaustion and a pounding headache left me no desire to engage in more pointless conversation. Rema's daughter slept in her arms while one of the boys, clearly bitter from earlier, turned to me.

"Do you know what happened to Meherdad?" he asked, with a smirk that held some twisted satisfaction. He continued without waiting for my response. "When he got lost at the airport, he ended up back at the motel. He got into a fight because he was drunk, and someone stabbed him to death. That's what no one else wanted to tell you—but I will."

My heart sank. I immediately asked him to call the smuggler from his phone. He resisted, but I raised my voice, insisting. He finally dialed the smuggler and passed me the phone.

"Where is Meherdad? What happened to him? Is what I heard true?" I asked, my voice trembling.

The smuggler's voice came through the line. "Yes, Meherdad got into a fight. He's injured, but I swear to my mother's life, he's alive and okay. It's late now, but I promise he will call you tomorrow." He must have sensed the panic in my voice. He reassured me again, "I swear he's okay. You'll see him soon."

I handed the phone back, and the smuggler must have scolded the boy, because I could hear him responding defensively, "I just wanted to be truthful. It's what I heard from others." The boy stayed quiet after that.

A bit of hope returned to me, enough for me to breathe again. Looking out the taxi window, I realized we were far from Jakarta, likely somewhere in a remote village or suburb. The boys had been chattering so incessantly that I hadn't even noticed how long we'd been driving. It had been hours, and I suspected we were nearing a new city, but I didn't know why. I didn't dare ask any of them, knowing their response might only worsen my anxiety.

Thankfully, the silence stretched on after the call. The driver stopped at a gas station, and while we waited, a familiar face approached our taxi. One of the men I'd seen at the hotel, who seemed more reasonable than the others, signaled for me to roll down the window. He explained, "At one of the gas stations, the police almost arrested us. We had to bribe them with a fair amount of money to avoid it." His face was pale, and I believed him—I'd seen how brutal the Indonesian police could be. He continued, "The smuggler wants to settle us in a remote village until the next departure."

He spoke calmly, and his demeanor was a welcome change from the others. Later, at the hotel, he told me his story: he was once a successful businessman but ended up associating with the wrong people. One of his debtors was highly influential in the government, and as a result, he lost everything. When it became clear he couldn't repay his debts and faced jail, he decided to leave the country.

When the driver returned, we resumed our journey, heading into streets that became increasingly narrow, almost like alleys—just wide enough for one car. Suddenly, a loud motorcycle approached from behind. Two large men got off and asked the young man in our taxi to leave. One of them took the young man away on the motorcycle, while the other climbed into our taxi. I gathered from their conversation that Rema and the other young man were familiar with him, likely having met before during the waiting period for our journey.

The man, with long blond hair and a beard, spoke to the driver fluently in the local language, indicating he'd been in Indonesia for quite some time. The driver followed his directions, taking us deeper into a maze of narrow streets. My heart pounded loudly, the uncertainty gnawed at me. The man looked at me and asked, "Are you Meherdad's aunt?" I nodded but said nothing.

"Why don't you answer? Are you scared?" he taunted, a mocking smile on his face. I replied simply, "I'm just very tired. Is Meherdad okay?"

He paused, then responded, "Yes, but it was close. He almost got us all in trouble. You'll see him in a few days." His words didn't comfort me. After all I'd witnessed so far, I found it impossible to trust anyone without seeing proof. This paranoia, even years later, remains ingrained in me.

Finally, the taxi stopped in front of a villa surrounded by other similar houses. The man paid the fare and led us inside, instructing us to be as quiet as possible since two other families were already sleeping. He showed us around briefly, mentioning he'd return to check on us in the coming days. The villa had one bedroom with two double beds and filthy bedding.

I went to wash my face in the bathroom, then found some eggs and stale bread in the kitchen. I quickly cooked the eggs and brought them back to the bedroom to share with Rema, while her daughter remained fast asleep. As I was eating, Rema said in her usual cheeky tone, "Mommy, can you find some rice too? I can't eat without rice." I looked at her with a wry smile and, while chewing, responded, "It seems I wasn't a good mother to you—I didn't teach you enough manners. But it's never too late if you're willing to learn." That ended our conversation, and we both finally surrendered to sleep. Despite everything, the dirty bed felt like a five-star hotel to me.

The next morning, I woke earlier than planned, startled by familiar voices in the hallway. I jumped up, hoping it was Meherdad, but it was the mechanic Ahmed, his family, and the young couple, Zara and Mohammad. It was comforting to see them again. I was glad they were our new housemates; at least they were much more reasonable compared to some of the others.

They explained that this villa was allocated for families, while singles were staying in different houses nearby. Thankfully, the smuggler had decided not to mix families with singles, which made me feel somewhat safer. Some of the singles' behaviors had been far from acceptable, even by loose social standards. At least here, we were with people who seemed more stable.

Ahmed suggested that he and Mohammad could handle the shopping for essentials, and we agreed that every evening we'd settle our share of the expenses. We also divided household chores amongst us, creating a routine. While the men went out to shop, I helped the other two women with preparations for daily necessities. For the first time, we sat down and had a proper conversation, getting to know one another a bit more personally.

That day passed peacefully. In the evening, the man who had brought us to the villa returned. It wasn't as dark this time, and I could see him better. Unlike the main smuggler, he was tall, big, and had a strong downtown accent, which he seemed to exaggerate for intimidation. He brought another woman with him, asking us to let her stay in the villa. She was slightly older than Rema, probably in her late thirties, with somewhat better manners, though not perfect. I soon realized she and Rema knew each other well, as they had argued before.

Her name was Fariba, and she was also going to sleep in our room. The man provided her with a small foldable bed, making the already crowded room even tighter. There wasn't much space left to walk around, and it was clear the room would now only be used for sleep. Sharing accommodation with all these people wasn't easy, but we all had hope that soon we'd be boarding and moving on from this place. The man reiterated, as usual, that we had to be ready at any moment for departure, with no specific date or time given.

I explained to Fariba the arrangements we'd made for food and household chores. She didn't argue, but she also didn't say much, and from that day onward, neither she nor Rema contributed to our shared responsibilities or expenses. Ahmed, the mechanic, reminded them a few times to pay their share, but they always avoided it.

Every evening, Rema and Fariba would leave for the disco, café, or tea house, meeting up with others from the singles' villa. They'd return late at night, sometimes even in the early morning. Ahmed, from a strict and religious family, warned them that if they continued coming back at midnight, he would lock them out, but they didn't seem to care. I advised Ahmed not to interfere too much; after all, we were temporary housemates and might never see each other again. It was clear we couldn't change their lifestyle, but he remained frustrated by their behavior.

One afternoon, after lunch, we all went to our rooms for a nap. Suddenly, I heard a strong voice—Meherdad's voice! I'll never forget seeing him again. It felt like he had been given a second chance at life, at least to me. He was there, alive, looking healthy, with the big man from the smuggler's crew standing next to him, smiling. The man said, "Here he is, a gift for you," and I completely forgot he wasn't really my nephew. I hugged Meherdad tightly, tears flowing, and everyone else gathered around us, also crying.

At that moment, I noticed even the big man was in tears. It wasn't just about Meherdad; it was about all of us missing the loved ones we had left behind. Whether it was political, social, or financial reasons that had driven us here, we had all left something or someone behind, unsure if we would ever see them again. Despite the hardships, nothing felt like home—no matter how grand a place might be, it could never replace one's own, even if it was a simple old cottage.

In contrast, Meherdad seemed happy, saying he had first been sent to the singles' villa but asked to be moved here. Initially, they had refused, but one of the smuggler's staff mentioned how worried I had been, always asking about him, and so they made an exception. They saw in my concern for Meherdad a reflection of their own mothers, left behind. It was an emotional reunion, and even now, years later, the memory brings tears to my eyes.

With Meherdad back, we began to explore the small province. Before, we'd only gone out for essentials, but now Meherdad encouraged us to enjoy the area. Along with Ahmed's son, Hamid, and the other women, we started venturing out every afternoon. There was a small internet café with many computers on short-legged tables, where we spent time playing games. I would also check my emails daily.

We explored the streets near the villa and occasionally took the funny minibusses further out, discovering beautiful areas around us, including a luxurious hotel with a large garden and three pools. Since the hotel appeared mostly empty, we took advantage of the garden and pools every day. It was a small comfort amid the uncertainties of our journey.

These new routines brought a bit of color to our otherwise dull days. Every evening after dinner, we played games, and I was happy that we were at least getting along well. The girls and Meherdad went out almost every evening, coming back very late, sometimes at dawn.

Ahmed and Mohammad didn't complain about Meherdad, but they couldn't stop criticizing the girls. Part of their frustration was that despite repeated warnings, the girls still hadn't contributed their share of expenses even once. I was covering the costs for both Meherdad and myself, and it was surprising that he didn't even mention it while everyone else assumed he was paying. He even borrowed money a few times, promising to pay it back, but that never happened.

We all had a limited amount of money, and if we were stuck here for a long time, as had happened to many others before us, it could spell trouble. The most frustrating part about the girls, though, wasn't their refusal to pay. It was the negativity they brought back from their nightly outings with the singles group—constantly repeating rumors about how bad things were going to be. They told us about a boat that had recently sunk, killing all its passengers. Despite my repeated requests and those of others to stop spreading such stories, they continued each morning.

I eventually complained to the big man when he visited one night, saying we were tired of all the negativity. He harshly warned the girls, even threatening to kick them out if they didn't stop. That was when I found out that neither of these two girls had paid the smuggler for their travel fees. I couldn't understand how they were allowed to stay.

One late afternoon, the big man arrived with two others and told us to be ready as we might soon be transferred. Mahdi was with him, and he said it was better for Mahdi to stay with us. He brought extra bedding for Mahdi, who would sleep on the floor where Meherdad usually slept. Personally, I was thrilled to see Mahdi again, but Rema, for reasons I couldn't fathom, seemed upset and kept teasing him, almost to the point of bullying.

From the big man's words, we all anticipated that the journey might soon continue, bringing a mix of excitement, fear, and worry. Conversations about the boat journey and all the details we had heard filled our gatherings. But days passed—more than a week—since he told us to be ready, and nothing happened.

One day, while the other two women and I were out shopping, taking one of those funny minibuses, we ran into Isa, a man we had seen during the broken boat episode. He had his little daughter with him, around seven or eight years old, without her mother. Isa told us he had been staying in the singles' villa, and that the previous night, a man from their group had died, and two others had gone blind. They had bought industrial alcohol as a beverage, and the consequences were tragic.

Isa explained why he had left the singles' villa. After the man died, the smuggler advised them to leave the body in front of the hospital, with the man's passport, so that his identity could be discovered. Isa couldn't stand to stay there with his daughter, especially with the body still present, so he left and asked if he could stay with us. I was astonished—how could he have ever been placed with the singles in the first place, especially with such a young child?

When we returned to our villa, the big man was there, speaking with Ahmed. He claimed that he and his men had taken care of the body and planned to send it back to Iran. No one dared to ask how that was possible. With all the difficulty they had transferring us, how could they arrange for the transport of a deceased man across international borders?

If he was telling the truth, their connections must be far deeper than we had thought, with access to high-level authorities. But there was another possibility—maybe they had simply disposed of the body, and were lying to us. Either way, we were not dealing with ordinary human traffickers; these men were skilled, calculated, and dangerous.

For the next few days, a heavy silence fell over us all. No one spoke much, and the nightly laughter and games stopped. Even Meherdad and the girls stayed in, no longer sneaking out after dark. It was as if we had all been snapped back to the grim reality of our situation. We had started to think of our stay as a strange kind of vacation, but the death of that young man reminded us just how serious and life-threatening this journey really was. Only Mahdi, Hamid, and the younger children spoke or played, their voices the only human sounds echoing in the villa. The sudden quiet must have puzzled even the neighbors who had complained about our noise.

The morning after breakfast, Meherdad asked me to join him in the garden. He said he had spoken with the smuggler, who had told him that another boat would be departing soon, and that we could be on it. He planned for us to leave, but it wouldn't include the others—not yet. He told me that when we went back inside, he would tell the group that we planned to make our own arrangements to leave. We would return to Jakarta and negotiate with the smuggler directly about the timing of our next departure.

When we went back inside, I began packing our few belongings while Meherdad spoke with the others. They weren't surprised but were visibly upset by our decision. They all had similar thoughts—many wanted to leave and find another smuggler—but feared that asking for their money back would cause trouble. The smuggler wasn't running a typical business; there were no guarantees, and making complaints could easily lead to losing everything, including their lives. For most of us, our visas had already expired, which made any confrontation with authorities even riskier.

Though the smuggler likely preferred to settle matters without unnecessary violence, it was clear that any serious objection could be met with severe consequences. He and his crew were working in an illegal field, and for people like them, there was no limit to the measures they might take to protect their interests.

We said our goodbyes to the others, with sadness and tears. I despised myself for lying to them. I had fled my country to escape being a corrupt liar, and now, for my own good, I had become just that. The smuggler had been adamant that we shouldn't tell anyone, especially since, after the death of the young man, the others were desperate to leave as soon as possible.

I was certain that nobody, except for those directly working for him, knew how his arrangements operated. It was clear, though, that he couldn't send everyone to the ocean at the same time. He claimed the weather and ocean conditions were the reason, but I doubted his words. After all, if safety was a real concern, how could so many boats still sink without change? There had to be something more—perhaps a deal with the authorities or another network involved.

We left the villa, our departure filled with a sense of guilt and uncertainty. It wasn't a remote area, but finding a taxi to Jakarta proved challenging. We walked a long distance to a road where vehicles might take us to other cities. Eventually, we found a cab, but the driver would only take us to a train station from where we could continue to Jakarta. Tired from our walk, we accepted.

Meherdad told me that he had run out of money but wasn't worried since he believed we'd be leaving for the ocean soon. I suspected his lack of concern had more to do with relying on me. Even back at the villa, when splitting expenses, he would always say, "You pay now, I'll repay you later." It surprised me that he had already used up all his money, even though he hadn't paid for anything on his own. The others assumed it was normal since they thought of him as my nephew, but I began to fear I wouldn't be able to keep playing the role of his generous aunt much longer.

Many traveled this way, expecting to leave Indonesia quickly, only to find themselves stuck for weeks or months, without a backup plan. I met a mother and daughter later who had been in Indonesia for several months with no money. They had handed all their savings over to the smuggler, who provided them with basic needs—but just enough to survive. Whether he did this out of a sense of humanity or simply to protect his reputation, I wasn't sure. But at least he hadn't abandoned them, unlike so many others I had heard about.

We were sitting on the hot, heavy bench at the train station, waiting for the next train, when Fariba called Meherdad. He put the call on speaker so I could listen too. Her tone wasn't surprising—far from friendly. She wanted to confirm if Meherdad had told her the truth. Meherdad, in his usual overly friendly voice, reassured her that we had no plans to continue with this smuggler. Instead, he explained that we were headed to Jakarta to get our money back and find another, safer smuggler. He even promised to share all the details once things were sorted. What a dirty game we were playing. Just yesterday, these people felt like family, and today, for our own survival, we had to betray them.

Since we left, Meherdad had received a few more calls and texts from the group, and he was great at deceiving them all. They called my phone too, but I didn't answer any of the calls. I advised him not to answer either, but he argued that ignoring them would raise suspicion. If they called the smuggler, he might get suspicious, and it could jeopardize our chances of leaving for the ocean, which could happen as soon as we got to Jakarta.

His words filled me with two overwhelming fears. First, the looming reality of our journey—a repeat of the horror we experienced last time—would happen again, possibly very soon. Just thinking about it was terrifying. Second, I realized how good Meherdad was at manipulating people. If the situation demanded it—whether for survival or personal gain—he would betray even me, his supposed "beloved auntie."

It was a bitter realization that this new generation seemed to lack the empathy my generation held dear. Perhaps it was a consequence of growing up in a place where survival demanded constant cunning. But now, years later, I see it differently. It wasn't just limited to countries like mine; it was happening everywhere. Individual survival and self-interest seemed to come before anything else, no matter the cost.

Chapter Eleven

I stayed silent on the train while Meherdad went on discussing the next steps we needed to take. My mind was elsewhere, replaying thoughts of the people we had left at the villa. I kept wondering if we would all manage to survive this journey, and if fate would ever allow us to see each other again. The uncertainty weighed heavily on my heart.

Once we arrived at the station, I was relieved to see taxis waiting—luckily, there wouldn't be another long walk ahead. We climbed into a taxi, and I told Meherdad that we needed to change some money to pay the driver. He suggested I could just use dollars, and the driver would give me the change, but I wasn't comfortable exposing my hidden money, especially not in front of Meherdad. I wanted to keep my secret stash just that—a secret.

I made an excuse. "Let's stop by one of those big hotels. They usually exchange currency at reception, and I also need to use the restroom." The taxi pulled over at a grand five-star hotel. These kinds of places were frequented by tourists, and I knew they'd likely exchange money without much hassle. Plus, it felt like a safer option.

Once inside, I went straight to the restroom. The money I retrieved from its hiding place was damp—ever since our first failed attempt on the boat, I hadn't found a moment alone long enough to properly dry it. I took out a $100 bill and approached the receptionist to exchange it. He immediately noticed the dampness of the note and gave me a look—a meaningful, almost sympathetic look, as if he understood everything I'd been through. Though the look made me uncomfortable and a bit embarrassed, I ignored it, received my change, and hurried back to the taxi.

The driver took us back to the same motel we had left before. Many people were still gathered around the pool, though not quite as many as last time. It made me wonder—perhaps some of them had already managed to depart, a thought that offered me a small glimmer of hope. We went directly to the room assigned to us by the smuggler, exhausted from the day's events. We needed rest before we could head out to buy the necessities for the journey that lay ahead.

The smuggler had assured us that our departure would happen soon, though we still had no idea exactly when. One thing we knew for certain from our last experience: it would definitely take place at night. So we still had a bit of time left. All the items we had bought last time—like sunscreen, anti-nausea medicine, vitamins, and snacks—had been used up during our stay in the villa or shared with others while we were on the boat.

After a few hours of rest, we decided to leave the motel to grab a proper meal and buy the essential items we would need. We had a decent meal, though I avoided eating at the local eateries around the motel. I didn't want to risk falling ill, given that food safety didn't seem to be a priority at those places—getting sick now would be disastrous. Instead, we opted for a nearby McDonald's. It might not have been the healthiest choice, but it felt safer and more familiar under the circumstances.

Shopping was done quickly since we knew exactly what we needed. Besides, I had to cover all the expenses, and the more time we spent shopping, the more money I would end up spending. Frankly, I wasn't too pleased about paying for everything, even if Meherdad were my real nephew—he should have been responsible for his own costs. I didn't mind helping out a few times, but doing it all the time felt unfair. There was no guarantee that we wouldn't face another situation like last time with the broken boat, which would force us to stay here longer, and I would need my savings. I didn't hesitate to make my thoughts clear, asking him, "What happened to your money? Didn't you have enough when you came here?"

His reaction was telling—he looked irritated, as though he hadn't expected his "auntie" to ask such a question. He replied, "I had a lot of money, but I shared it with those who didn't have any." It was a blatant lie, and given what I knew of his personality, I found it hard to believe he'd spend his money like that without a reason.

When we got back to the motel, he left almost immediately. The silence between us following my question suggested that he didn't appreciate being confronted. After he left to meet his friends, I sat alone in front of the TV. It wasn't very late in the afternoon when the door suddenly burst open without any warning—something you learn to expect here. One of the smuggler's workers entered with two young couples, announcing that they would be staying in our room.

Sherri and her husband Reza, and Lili and her husband Arya, all seemed to be around their late twenties. Sherri and Reza looked relaxed and happy, while Lili, a strikingly beautiful woman with a loose hijab, seemed visibly anxious and scared. Her obvious distress caught my attention, and I found myself asking why she was so afraid. She leaned back on her friend for support and asked me questions about how the whole process would unfold. I shared whatever I knew.

They mentioned they had only just arrived the previous night—Reza, his cousin Arya, and Sherri had come a night earlier, and Lili had just joined them. It was clear they knew each other from before, all coming from the same suburb as Meherdad in Tehran. I told them about Meherdad, that he was also with me, and that he was out but would join us later. I also advised them about the essential items they needed to buy, as the only thing they had brought was a lot of dry nuts.

Reza's cousin had traveled with the same smuggler six months ago and was now living in Perth. He had recommended this route to Sherri and Reza, who in turn had advised Arya and Lili. We were still in the middle of that conversation when Meherdad came back. He wasn't at all surprised to see the new couples and quickly got friendly with them. The men decided to go out for the necessary shopping and buy ingredients to cook dinner, while the women and I stayed in the room.

After they left, Lili came over to me while I was preparing some food in the kitchen. She confided, "We're not really a married couple. Arya isn't even my boyfriend—I just said we were married so I'd feel safer." I wasn't sure why she was telling me this, but I could understand why someone as beautiful as she was might feel vulnerable traveling this way.

When the men returned, we all had dinner together. Everyone seemed cheerful, and Lili was finally laughing, her earlier fears seemingly gone. They started playing games, and Meherdad suggested they visit an internet gaming café nearby to play computer games, which everyone seemed excited about. I didn't know anything about computer games, but it was better than staying alone in the room.

The café was just across the street from the motel. Despite the late hour, the city felt alive, with bustling crowds and many cars—a comforting sight. While they played, I sat there feeling bored and decided to head back to the room before them. Hours later, they returned, their loud laughter carrying through the hall. Lying in my room, I could hear them joking and playing games until late into the night. Despite needing rest, I couldn't bring myself to be upset with them—their youthful energy brought some much-needed joy to this dreary place. I only hoped that they'd settle down soon, as I longed for peace.

Finally, they decided to go to bed. The girls joined me in one room, while the boys slept in the other. Even after the lights went out, it took me a while to fall asleep with all the noise still echoing in my mind.

So, it didn't happen that night. The next day, I was the first one awake, followed gradually by everyone else. We didn't have much to do except wait—waiting for something monumental to happen, without knowing when, was incredibly draining, especially with little to distract our minds. The men left to buy groceries for our next meal, and the girls started chatting while I kept myself occupied with the TV. Occasionally, they would ask me questions about my previous boat experience, but I had already shared everything I knew.

Later, when the boys returned, we prepared something to eat. Sitting on the floor, it felt as if we had all known each other for a long time. They chatted and laughed, and it was genuinely heartwarming to witness. The only one who seemed uneasy was Arya, likely because Lili was making it clear to everyone that they were not married. I understood why she initially claimed he was her husband—to feel protected—but why she decided to drop that facade now was less obvious. Perhaps she felt more secure or had found another source of support, but it was clear she no longer wanted Arya around her.

The men had met one of the smuggler's staff during their shopping trip and invited him to come by our room later, hoping to gather some useful information. Eventually, he knocked on the door, and I was thankful for once that someone was actually knocking before entering. He was a young man in his early thirties, visibly frail and thin. The way he spoke and moved indicated he wasn't in good health. I couldn't understand how he had ended up working for the smuggler, as I'd imagined smugglers' employees to be physically strong and imposing. Then, he explained his story: many of the smuggler's staff were former passengers who, for various reasons, could not complete the journey—whether they had been arrested, fallen ill, or simply run out of money. Since they couldn't or didn't want to return home, they worked for the smuggler to cover their expenses, helping out in whatever capacity they could.

I wondered if he knew more personal details about the smuggler, but as if reading my mind, he said, "Only a few of us really know the smuggler closely. Most don't even know where he lives or his real name. He gives different names to different people to keep them compartmentalized." I had heard this before, so at least part of what he was saying was true.

He said he planned to leave with the next group but had been working for the smuggler because his illness had drained his finances. He had been there for several months but had finally earned enough to pay his way forward. I was curious about what he could possibly do for the smuggler, given his frail condition. He explained, "I do exactly what I'm doing now—go from room to room and answer everyone's endless questions, keeping the smuggler from dealing with his clients directly."

I had to admit, the smuggler seemed smarter than I had thought. Staying away from disgruntled clients likely prevented conflicts and kept the operation running smoothly. Angry customers could cause significant problems, including exposing the smuggler's activities to the authorities. The only other rumor I had heard was that they dealt with troublesome clients in the harshest ways possible—a possibility I hoped was false.

He stayed with us for some time, even joining us for afternoon tea. While I didn't find his information particularly useful, the others were eager to absorb everything he said, as they had no prior experience like mine. He kept assuring us that the journey would be safe, with the best boats, plenty of food and water, and carefully chosen routes with all safety measures in place. It was nonsense—I had just returned from one of these "safe" boats that had broken down halfway through the journey.

He didn't seem to like my questions or challenges and kept making excuses, claiming that my experience was an exception. I noticed the others weren't thrilled with my questioning either; their glances and responses made it clear they didn't appreciate the doubt I was casting. Now that they had made their decision, they didn't want anyone heightening their fears, even if it was the truth. I could understand their perspective—after all, I had felt the same frustration when those two girls in the villa were sharing negative stories.

Everyone here had committed to this journey, despite the terrifying possibility of drowning in the ocean. No one wanted to dwell on it or, worse, hear it discussed openly. We all had our reasons, and each of us was willing to pay whatever the cost to reach our destination.

The proof of this statement lies in the experiences of people who ended up in Nauru and never returned home. They chose to endure years of imprisonment rather than face what awaited them back home—something far worse. I truly don't understand how this simple fact doesn't prove that they deserve asylum. Instead, they've been left in limbo, in unacceptable conditions for so many years.

When he left, it was already dark. Everyone seemed somewhat relieved by the reassurances he had given. Reza spoke loudly to his wife, Sherrin, "See? I told you there's nothing to worry about." Shortly after, Meherdad received a call—both of us needed to move upstairs to another room. We immediately knew what that meant. An uncomfortable silence settled over the group; the others could sense we were about to leave and didn't like the idea of being left behind. We said our goodbyes, though the look in their eyes showed they wished to join us. Lili asked if we were departing that night, and though I said I didn't know, her heavy gaze showed she suspected I wasn't telling the truth. Moving us could mean a lot, but there were no guarantees.

Once the door to our new room opened, we saw a crowd of mostly single travelers gathered around. The smuggler himself was there, greeting me with a smile, "Auntie, go ahead inside." In the room were other families—a visibly angry woman in her late forties, with her two children, both in their twenties. The daughter, Gelareh, was on her phone, silently crying, while her mother kept urging her to hang up. The son, Razi, was the calmest of the three, trying to soothe his mother and sister.

The mother did not hold back her resentment; it was obvious that this journey was not her choice nor her daughter's. Her son seemed to have been the one pushing for it. She didn't miss any opportunity to show her frustration, not only making it evident through her words but also projecting it onto others. In such a tense situation, staying quiet was the best option—everyone was under enough stress already, and there was no point in making things worse. This was no ordinary flight where you could ask the stewardess to change your seat. People react differently under pressure, and understanding that was key to surviving this journey.

As I was lost in thought, I suddenly heard the smuggler's loud, welcoming voice, followed by Reza's cheerful greeting. I moved from the bed, joining the others, and saw Reza and Sherri entering the room with big smiles. It seemed they would be joining us after all.

The smuggler divided us into two groups—singles and families—and appointed a leader for each. Meherdad was assigned as the leader for the families. He then sent Arya to join the singles group. Arya protested, insisting that Lili was his wife and he wanted to stay with the families, but the smuggler's voice exploded in anger: "If you or anyone else doesn't listen to me or your leader, we will shoot you in the ocean." Arya backed down and reluctantly joined the singles, while Lili laughed quietly.

I wondered how the smuggler knew Arya and Lili weren't truly married. We hadn't shown any IDs, yet Lili had apparently informed the smuggler herself that Arya wasn't her husband, and she wanted distance. It was strange, given she had initially told me otherwise, but I chose not to dwell on her motives.

The smuggler's threat was likely more about setting an example and maintaining control, ensuring everyone knew that dissent wouldn't be tolerated. While I had observed the travelers gossiping and poking fun at each other during our stay in the motel, no real conflicts had surfaced. But I could imagine that under the extreme conditions of the ocean, things could easily escalate. This threat felt both precautionary and indicative of the kind of situations they might have faced before.

When I decided on this journey, I knew I had to prepare myself for anything—strange, scary, and unpredictable. I'd been focused on fearing the smugglers, but it hadn't occurred to me that some of the travelers themselves could be dangerous. Still, it was too late to rethink things now.

Even if I had known earlier, I wouldn't have given up my dream just because of potential threats. I reminded myself that I was determined not to turn back, no matter the cost. If anything happened, I would stand for what I believed in until my last breath.

We stepped out with our bags, and the smuggler turned his anger on the visibly upset mother in our group, yelling, "Didn't I tell you to bring only a small bag? Do you want me to leave you here?" She said nothing, looking terrified, while her daughter muttered under her breath. I felt for her—they were already overwhelmed with fear, and now she was being publicly humiliated. It wasn't just her; his demeaning attitude made us all feel small, reduced to people desperately needing his favor. No one dared to challenge him; everyone kept silent, whether out of fear or resignation.

This sense of superiority he carried, without any real merit, reminded me of the people I had worked with back home—people who lorded their positions over others. But at least with the smuggler, this was temporary. Once I reached my destination, he would become a dark memory I could finally leave behind, replaced by the hope of freedom and a new life. While my dignity was certainly bruised, there was still hope for healing in the future that lay ahead.

We were instructed to leave the room in groups of eight. I was definitely part of the family group, with Meherdad leading us. No further instructions were given, except that a van would be waiting for each group at the motel door. We were told to act as normal as possible, even avoiding the other travelers in the motel who were still waiting for their own departure.

We left quietly, not all together. A small white van waited for us, its driver showing his wide smile filled with big, stained teeth, silently pointing for us to get in. Without a word, we obeyed. Meherdad, Razi, and the driver took the front seats, while Reza, Sherri, and Lili sat in the second row, leaving me, Gelareh, and her mother in the last row.

As the van started moving, I thought perhaps we would make part of the journey by plane, but I quickly realized I was wrong. There would be no airport this time—just an endless drive into uncertainty. The driver, who knew no English and barely seemed to understand us, drove recklessly for nearly twenty-four hours, stopping only for brief moments to let us use a restroom or stretch our legs. We asked him questions, even using gestures, but all he gave in response was his constant smile, revealing his stained teeth. It was clear he had no intention of telling us anything.

His driving was terrifying—speeding carelessly, as though we were cargo instead of human beings. I was seated by the window, and more than once I hit my head against the glass, once so hard it left me with a headache for hours. He also smoked inside the van without any concern for us, ignoring our protests with that same grin. Eventually, we gave up trying to reason with him. The smuggler had warned us not to contact him or his staff unless there was an emergency. Otherwise, he would have us left wherever we were—no questions asked. None of us doubted he was serious.

After a grueling twenty-four hours, late at night, the driver pulled over in the middle of a forest. The surroundings were as remote and eerie as before, though I doubted it was the same place as last time—surely, the smugglers changed routes to avoid detection. Everyone in the van was scared and reluctant to get out. But, having been through this before, I reassured them that we would soon meet others. It was pitch dark, the only light coming from the full moon above. As soon as the driver dropped us off, he left without a word.

I led the way, calming the others, and soon enough, we heard whispering—another group merging with us, just as I had expected. The moonlight, though dim, occasionally gave us glimpses of each other's faces. I felt much calmer this time since I had an idea of what was coming next. The only worry was my still-healing foot, which might not hold up well under the strain of another long walk. Lili stayed close to me, her face filled with fear. I reassured her, and I could see some of her tension lift as she began to trust me.

As we walked, I wondered just how many people were in our group. If more were to join later, we would be a massive number—much larger than last time. Could the boat even handle this many people? And what if it broke down again, only this time further out at sea, too far to be rescued? Even breaking down close to shore again would be unbearable.

I had heard that some people who went through similar ordeals in the past gave up and returned home, lucky just to be alive. Others weren't as fortunate. But there was no point in dwelling on those fears now—it was too late. All that mattered was reaching the STOP as quickly as possible. Everyone seemed to share the same thought, focused only on being the first to get there.

We were told, just like last time, that when we reached the STOP, small boats would be waiting to take us to a larger boat. But, we'd still need to walk through water to get to them since even the small boats couldn't anchor right on the shore. I already knew all of this, and I had shared these details with the others earlier. This time, my previous experience made the journey a bit easier, even though my knee still ached from the last walk. I knew there would be no Mahdi to rescue me now, and honestly, I didn't expect anyone here to look out for anyone but their own family when things got tough. It was harsh but entirely understandable.

Suddenly, one of the boys ahead of us yelled, "There it is—STOP! I can see it!" He was walking a bit further ahead of everyone else. At first, I thought he might be mistaken because I remembered the walk being longer last time. It was dark, so I couldn't make out my surroundings well, but I could tell this wasn't the same forest as before.

Later, I heard from the others that it was the "General"—the man I had spoken to on the phone—who directed the smuggler which routes to take. Since he was connected with the police, he supposedly knew when and where they would be patrolling, allowing him to find us a safer route. But even though we heard all these assurances, nothing was truly guaranteed. There were too many stories of people being arrested at the very last moment, right when they were finally boarding the boats. We all knew we still had to be careful—no loud noises or bright lights that might give away our position to the authorities.

Finally, we could see both the small boats and the larger boat, its lights illuminating the area. I found it strange that the lights were on, but maybe they were confident this route was safe tonight. We were about 700 meters from the larger boat, and several smaller boats were anchored closer to shore, though not close enough to walk directly onto them. We had to wade through the water.

It felt like everything was going more smoothly this time, though maybe it was just because I knew what to expect, and that made it easier to handle. I wasn't sure exactly how many of us were there, but we were enough that the small boats would have to make several trips to carry everyone to the larger boat. We started boarding the small boats. Though each was built to hold about 7-8 people at most, we were crammed in, far beyond that capacity.

Suddenly, I saw Selma and her daughter Mina—the mother and daughter I had met during my last attempt. Mina, despite this being her third experience, was still visibly terrified, clinging to her mother and crying. The tension and fear were palpable, and her loud sobs cut through the night air.

Next to me in the small boat was Lili. As she tried to climb aboard, she misplaced her foot in the dark and fell badly into a hole in the boat. She screamed in pain, and when she pulled up her pants leg, I could see she had a bleeding cut—not deep, but clearly painful. She was crying, and I felt a pang of sorrow for her. I wrapped my arms around her, trying to comfort her as best as I could, holding her tightly as she cried.

The entire situation seemed overwhelming, but somehow, having someone else to care for in that moment—just like with Mahdi last time—helped me feel a bit stronger, as if, by comforting Lili, I could also quiet my own fears.

I don't know whether I hugged Lili for her sake or if I needed it just as much. Whatever the reason, her sobbing in my arms brought out my own tears. Why were we so desperate to leave our homes and lives behind like this? I could feel her tears soaking into my chest, and I held her tighter, hoping that the warmth of the embrace could share the burden between us, even for just a moment.

Next to us was a man in his late 40s, his young wife Sara, and their two children, maybe aged three and five. Everyone seemed to know him, calling him by his surname. The children were crying loudly, clinging to their mother, while the man tried to wrap his arms around all of them at once, a futile but heartfelt gesture. It was heartbreaking to see the kids so terrified, likely more from the shouts and cries of others than from the situation itself.

I couldn't help but wonder what would drive a parent to put their children through this ordeal. I understood, on some level, why he chose this—why I chose this. The choice wasn't about risking their physical lives; it was about the quality of their existence. Staying behind meant survival without the dignity of truly living. It meant being alive but never being able to truly live. As a parent, maybe it was his duty to take the risk, to teach his children that life is worth fighting for, even if it's terrifying. The idea of staying safe, yet living without freedom, seemed like an existence without purpose, like being a doll in a toy house.

I remembered a saying I once heard: "If you always watch your steps carefully, you may never fall, but you'll also never see the beauty of the sky." Maybe this journey was about leaving fear behind, even if it meant we could fall.

As we approached the larger boat, I could see we needed to climb a ladder to get aboard. The challenge of pulling myself up returned—an old fear I hadn't yet conquered. The boat had three levels, each one stacked above the other. The topmost level was open, with just a flimsy wooden guardrail, barely enough to hold anyone steady. The second level was deeper, closer to the engine and dwelling area, filled with heavy smoke from the fuel but offering some shelter from the elements. The lowest level, the main deck, was larger but still inadequate to hold everyone comfortably.

Family groups were assigned to the top and middle levels. I initially chose the top, but the boat's violent swaying made me rethink that decision. I couldn't keep myself steady there, so I decided to move to the second level, even though the engine's poisonous fumes filled the air. It was still better than the constant, terrifying motion of the top deck.

Even getting on board was a challenge. The boat wasn't designed for passengers like us—it was meant for sailors who could easily jump and navigate the narrow fences. For me, and the two other middle-aged women, it was a struggle. Others managed it effortlessly, like feathers in the wind, but I had to try several times, each time failing. I needed someone to push me up, just like last time. I was surprised that I didn't even feel embarrassed anymore—how could I still care about maintaining dignity in a moment like this?

The man in his late 40s managed to help me up, and I found a spot near the engine. It was far from ideal, but in that moment, I knew that being practical was more important than pride. As I got in the boat, I realized just how much had changed in me. The old version of myself would never have allowed such vulnerability, but here, surrounded by strangers in the middle of the sea, survival had a way of stripping away everything unnecessary.

First level with its terrifying swings, even before the boat started sailing, was something I knew I couldn't handle. I hadn't shown signs of seasickness the first time, but the intensity of the rocking this time had me worried. Everyone was clinging tightly to the narrow wooden railings to keep from falling, but it was almost impossible for me to do the same, unlike the others who seemed to manage better. In the middle of all the noise and commotion, I asked one of the young men to help me move down to the second level, which seemed a bit less daunting.

Now in the second level of the deck, surrounded by other families, I leaned my exhausted body against the engine room wall. Meherdad was with us too, but I noticed he seemed restless, eventually moving back up to the first level. Beside me sat another beautiful young woman, Azar, with short hair and a chubby figure. She was crying, worried that she had lost her husband back in the forest. I tried to reassure her, telling her, "Don't worry. Groups are still joining us; he's probably among the next to arrive. Just try to take a rest."

My clothes were soaked, like everyone else's, but it was the least of my concerns. As I comforted Azar, I suddenly realized I couldn't see my bag. I had handed it to someone when they were helping me climb up. Someone nearby assured me that once everyone was safely on board, all the bags would be handed out to their owners. Still, I felt uneasy; I had bottles of water in that bag, and my throat was parched.

More than thirst, though, I was overcome by sheer exhaustion. It had been over 48 hours without sleep, and even before we left, I hadn't rested properly. Sleeping in the cramped van was impossible, and every time I was about to doze off, the driver's reckless movements would jolt me awake, my head banging against the window.

Even as I spoke to Azar, leaning my head back against the wall, the exhaustion finally took over. The noise of the boat, the cries of the others, the movement around me—it all faded into the background as I drifted off, passing out from sheer fatigue. I must have slept for about an hour, maybe less, and it felt like the deepest sleep I'd had in days.

When I woke up, the boat was packed to the brim. People were crammed into every available space; it was far beyond capacity. The smuggler had filled it with as many passengers as he could. More people meant more money for him, but I couldn't help worrying. Would the boat be able to bear this weight? With so many onboard, the idea of the boat breaking down—like the last time—seemed more real than ever. And if it did break, hopefully it would be close to shore again, but if it wasn't, the outcome was unimaginable.

Azar sat next to me, and thankfully her husband had made it onto the boat, so they were reunited. I looked around with open eyes, trying to take in the scene and found my bag beside me. It seemed like someone had returned everyone's bags, but mine was almost empty—most of the water bottles and the food I had prepared for the journey were missing. I felt a pang of worry knowing we could be at sea for 7-8 days, at the very least.

The smuggler had told us we were heading to Darwin, a city in Australia's Northern Territory, which was a much further journey compared to other destinations like Christmas Island. I had heard that Christmas Island, which isn't technically in Australia, was leased by the Australian government to process asylum seekers, often with harsher conditions.

Among us, it was a common belief that landing in Darwin instead of Christmas Island meant a better chance of being granted permanent residency faster. It seemed that was why the smuggler had charged extra for those opting for Darwin, though I didn't understand how it made a difference to him. The extra charge didn't come with any additional service; instead, it was us who had to endure more hardships for that route.

Most members of the family group settled on the third level with its narrow fence. Many of them complained about the engine smoke in the cabin but came down whenever it rained or if the boat hit a storm, which happened quite often. I stayed in the cabin alongside Selma, her daughter Mina, and the man with his two young children—Kaviyani and his wife Sara. People addressed him by his surname, Kaviyani, which gave him a sense of respect or authority, but his children were clearly struggling with the cramped and unsafe conditions.

He frequently moved between levels, trying to balance the smoke of the cabin against the precariousness of the upper level, always doing his best to protect his family. I had heard whispers that the smuggler had kept him waiting in Indonesia for a long time. There were rumors that they had had multiple arguments, and this delay was the smuggler's way of punishing him. Given what I had seen with the girls in the villa, I had no reason to doubt it.

The boat was cramped, with an Indonesian captain, an older man in his late fifties, and two younger crew members, one in his twenties and the other barely an adult—may be 16 or 17. The youngest clearly wasn't an experienced sailor and appeared to be there just to help with smaller tasks.

Eventually, the engine roared to life, and the boat began to move, cutting through the dark water. We had officially set sail, and the realization was both terrifying and relieving. The tension of waiting had lifted, and everyone on board began praying loudly. For a brief moment, there were smiles—an odd mix of hope, relief, and the happiness of having made it this far despite all the obstacles. But the smiles were tinged with unease, as everyone knew that harder moments were coming soon.

The smoke from the engine filled the cabin, making it difficult to breathe, but I chose to stay where I was. The thought of that unstable upper level, with its flimsy, narrow fence, was scarier to me than the thick, acrid smoke. I saw that others were managing better than I was, but I couldn't help it. I preferred the suffocating safety of the cabin to the exposed terror above.

Outside the cabin, there was a narrow walkway on both sides, leading to two rickety ladders. One went down to where all the singles were crowded into the lower deck, and the other went up to the exposed upper level where most of the family group sat. Occasionally, someone from the family group would come into the cabin for a bit of respite, but the smoke soon drove them back out. I could hear them coughing and grumbling, and it only reminded me of the choices we had to make: endure the smoke, or face the fearsome rocking of the boat. Neither was an easy option.

People were talking loudly, discussing their thoughts and expectations for the journey ahead. The air was filled with nervous energy as we sailed on, leaving behind the forest, the walking, the long hours of anticipation. I tried to focus on the steady hum of the engine, hoping it would lull me into some sense of peace. The reality, though, was clear: we were out in the open ocean, with no turning back.

The boat's narrow passages were cluttered with large barrels of petrol, which strangely made it somewhat easier to navigate between the levels by using the barrels for support. We had been on the boat for a few hours by now, my clothes still damp but no longer uncomfortable. They would eventually dry out, and the temperature wasn't cold enough to be unbearable.

Soon, the need to use the toilet came, and the idea of maneuvering through all those petrol barrels and the tightly packed people along the corridor was daunting. I'd been dealing with continence issues since my first pregnancy, and this was one of my biggest worries from the beginning. On typical outings, I would limit my drinking, but on a journey expected to last over a week, limiting fluids wasn't an option. The cabin was unpleasant with the engine's poisonous fumes, but being closer to the toilet was a small comfort.

It took me a lot of effort to navigate through the obstacles to reach the toilet. I think I may have been the first one to try it, and it was a cramped, uncomfortable place—two wooden walls on each side, completely open on the front, which faced the ocean. The only thing separating me from the water was an old, tattered curtain that provided very little privacy.

There were no proper facilities, just three narrow planks of wood covering the floor, with a gap in the middle where everything would fall directly into the ocean below. There was no bowl, no tank, no toilet paper, and certainly no sanitation—nothing except a hose that pumped oily water, perhaps a discharge from the engine, that we were expected to use for washing. The lack of basic amenities was appalling, especially with children on board.

When I returned, everyone wanted to know about the toilet conditions. Clearly, I wasn't the only one worried about this. I described the bare essentials of what I'd seen. I washed my hands using that oily water, and though I nearly threw up from the smell and texture, I reminded myself to be grateful for any small comfort in this dire situation.

Navigating the tight passage back to the cabin was exhausting. When I finally got there, I saw Selma and Mina eating some warm food. My surprise turned into curiosity—how could they have hot food here? That's when I noticed one of the boys serving hot noodles from the deck. Apparently, the smuggler had provided some basic supplies, and a small group was in charge of distributing it. It was a luxury I hadn't expected. I asked for a smaller portion, just half of what they were serving, to which the boy responded with a confused but friendly smile. I supposed he thought I was watching my figure in such a situation—something so absurd it almost made me laugh bitterly.

Several of the boys had taken charge of distributing what food and water the smuggler provided. The water ration was just one-third of a glass per person per day, and it wasn't enough, but there was no option for more. The food consisted of a few basics, including boxes of eggs. However, when they opened them, a strong rotten smell wafted out, and all the eggs were promptly thrown overboard.

I later found out there were rumors circulating that the boys responsible for distributing food were hoarding the best parts for themselves—claims about energy drinks, dates, honey, and more. I hadn't believed it until one night, unable to sleep as usual, I saw them with my own eyes indulging in items none of us had received.

Being so close to the food storage area, I overheard more than a few murmurs of discontent. It was inevitable that, in a situation of scarcity, accusations and complaints would arise. One day, it finally happened—a group confronted the boys over the unequal distribution. One of the boys, big and imposing, shut them down quickly, practically bullying them into silence, saying that if they complained, they might not even get what little they were currently receiving. It was a raw display of power that showed me just how fragile our situation was.

These dynamics—people turning on each other in times of scarcity—were predictable. I had hoped that things wouldn't descend into chaos, especially where women and children were concerned, but I knew that desperation could bring out the worst in people. I kept praying that no further emergencies would push us to a breaking point where survival became a battle against one another. In this place, nothing would surprise me anymore, and that very thought was both a source of strength and a chilling realization.

Chapter Twelve

Seeing everyone enjoying their cups of hot noodles, which would have seemed unimpressive in any other situation, made me realize how our perceptions of "luxury" had drastically shifted. The warmth of the salty broth penetrated my entire being, providing a moment of comfort amidst the chaos. After each meal, they were generous enough to give each of us a third of a glass of water—an amount that brought an inexplicable joy to me as I savored every last sip.

As I looked up while drinking, my eyes caught the view in front of me where the captain was steering the boat. It was a beautiful day, with the bright sun casting a golden glow over the expansive blue ocean. It could have been a view to stir poetic emotions if the circumstances were different. Instead, it just reminded me of how far we still had to go, how we were only just beginning this arduous journey.

The realization that we had survived our first night at sea hung heavily in the air. The families from the upper level, who were struggling with the loose and precarious fences, joined us for their meal. Despite the smoke, they found a momentary refuge in the cabin. Among them were Razi's mother and her daughter, Gelareh, who continued to wear the same perpetually angry and disapproving expressions. Gelareh was eating only a piece of dry bread—the only thing her body could handle due to her abdominal issues. It was heartbreaking, and I knew that her struggle was only going to get worse as food supplies dwindled.

Meanwhile, something else caught my attention: a growing spark between Meherdad and Lili. It was evident from their exchanged glances and hidden smiles that a connection had formed. In such dire circumstances, perhaps the comfort of a sudden relationship was what they both needed—something to escape into, even momentarily. They both seemed lighter and happier, the gravity of our situation not touching them as deeply, at least for now.

Sherri and Reza, who had always been close to Lili, seemed to enjoy their new dynamic as a pair of couples, treating the situation like an adventure, even a holiday. Their constant jokes and teasing were infectious, and for a while, it lightened the mood for others around them.

However, there was a downside to this behavior. Sometimes, they overdid it—pushing the forced merriment too far, which grated on the nerves of those not in the mood for such levity. Razi's mother, already frustrated and uncomfortable, was particularly irritated by their behavior, and she continued to complain frequently. But her complaints only earned her more disrespect, both subtle and overt. The unspoken rule here was that complaints would not change anything; they would only make you a target for rudeness and exclusion. It wasn't a situation where logic or fairness would prevail.

Arya, who had been relegated to sitting in the passageway, was dealing with terrible seasickness from the very beginning. His condition was the worst of anyone on board, and it persisted throughout the entire journey. He barely spoke or interacted with anyone, as he was constantly hunched over, nauseated.

In contrast, Kaviyani and his wife Sara were doing their best to manage their children. Sara, despite her own discomfort, remained quietly focused on feeding the kids, keeping them entertained, and shielding them from the tension. Kaviyani, for his part, was demanding and gruff with everyone except his children, for whom he showed remarkable patience and care. It was clear that the other passengers did not particularly like his demeanor, as he expected constant support from everyone else, even though he himself rarely offered any.

As we were eating, Sara's younger child, carefree in his innocence, suddenly asked his mother, "Are we going to die tonight?" His words hit us all like an arrow to the heart. Even the boys distributing food paused and looked at the poor child with a mixture of pity and pain. I quickly hugged the boy and handed him a candy from my bag, hoping to cheer him up. He squirmed out of my embrace, saying, "I don't want you to kiss me. I want Lili to kiss me."

Lili smiled warmly at the boy, bending down to plant a kiss on his forehead. "I'll give you another kiss, but only if you promise never to ask that question again," she said gently. Her playful but heartfelt response brought a small smile to the boy's face, and it seemed to ease the tension, if only for a moment.

It was in these small moments—amidst the laughter, the tears, the fear, and the tenderness—that I realized how much we all needed each other. The connection we found in comforting one another was perhaps the only thing that kept us from being consumed entirely by the immense uncertainty surrounding us.

The bright sky and calm ocean made it easier for all of us to find a brief moment of peace. It had been almost a full day since we set sail, and somehow, it felt comforting to know that with each passing hour, we were closer to whatever destination awaited us. The captain was focused on steering, while his two assistants moved around the boat, tending to their tasks.

Some of the passengers, reassured by the daylight, began to drift off to sleep. I wanted to join them, but the fear of an emergency kept me awake. I had anti-stress and sleeping pills in my bag, but I knew it would be unwise to use them now. Instead, I leaned my head against the cabin wall, wrapping myself in the thickest piece of clothing I had brought along. My clothes were few, but I had packed what I thought might protect me from the winter chill that the ocean could bring.

By the second night, the storm had started. The boat moved like a feather, swaying wildly up and down. Those on the upper deck later shared how the boat was tossed so violently that they could almost touch the water. Whenever the storm hit, the families on the first level would come down to the cabin, seeking a bit more stability. During the worst moments, we would hold each other's hands, forming a circle around the children in an attempt to protect them. The children, in turn, were kept in the middle of the group, guarded by their parents and some of the younger men.

Despite our efforts, bodies were thrown against the cabin walls each time the boat took a deep dive or a sudden lurch. The screams were deafening—some were cries of fear, while others called out loudly for divine help, invoking spiritual guidance to keep us safe. There were even heated arguments when some accused others of not praying enough, believing that a lack of collective devotion was putting us all at greater risk. It was human nature—searching for someone to blame when faced with the uncontrollable forces of nature.

In those terrifying nights, at least the children slept, and that was one small mercy. They were often in their mother's arms, comforted enough to slip into dreams. Selma and her daughter Mina kept mostly to themselves. Mina eventually found her place among Lili, Gelareh, Azar, and Sherri.

They all had their moments of laughter and whispered conversations despite the situation. Even Gelareh, with her usual sullen expression, could occasionally be seen joining in their jokes.

In the calmer moments, we had a chance to talk, to connect, even if it was just to pass the time. Selma, Razi's mother, and I would sit together and share stories, though Razi's mother mostly listened with that same, perpetually disapproving look on her face. There were many moments when she wiped her tears in silence. She hadn't chosen this journey for herself or Gelareh—she had done it for Razi. Her love for her son had made her choose this uncertain path, unwilling to leave him alone. It was a common story in our country; a mother's sacrifice for her son, sometimes at the cost of her own happiness and that of her daughters.

Razi's mother's inner struggle was clear. She had given up everything she had worked for throughout her life to keep her son safe. She dragged Gelareh along, believing that was her duty as a mother. It was the tragedy of many Iranian women, sacrificing their dreams for the sake of others. Sons were often elevated above daughters in value, and the result was a cycle that kept repeating itself—one generation giving way to the next without challenging these deep-seated inequalities. For some women, conforming to these expectations, sacrificing freedom and dignity, was simply easier than facing the fear of standing up to the system.

When the ocean was calm, we shared our stories openly. We even indulged in gossip, though everyone was careful not to go too far. Selma told me about Kaviyani, the man with the two children. She said that she had known him since they had both arrived in Jakarta, and that his rude behavior wasn't new—he had treated others poorly from the start. One of the young men from the singles group once confided in me that Kaviyani had had several altercations with the smuggler himself. Apparently, the smuggler had warned that if Kaviyani caused too much trouble during the journey, he should be thrown into the ocean, even in front of his family. It sounded extreme, and no one really believed it would come to that, but it spoke to the tension that simmered just below the surface.

On calmer nights, when the ocean was peaceful, we sometimes gathered in the narrow passageway under the stars, sharing stories as a way of coping. The conversations flowed freely, and people swapped places to get to know each other better. I didn't often join in, but I could hear everything from my place in the cabin. Everyone called me "Auntie," as Meherdad had introduced me that way from the beginning. It was easy to tell that my presence made some of them think of their mothers—something they sorely missed. Even Kaviyani, who was harsh with most, showed me respect.

One night, as we sat in the passage near the barrels—most of which were now empty, having been thrown overboard—Kaviyani opened up to me. He said, "I'm not as horrible as they all think I am. But here, I want them to fear me. I want them to know that I'm a strong protector for my family." I tried to understand his reasoning. Perhaps, in his mind, being feared was the only way he knew how to protect his family, to ensure their safety in a world that offered so little of it.

The bright sky and the peaceful ocean lulled us all into a sense of fleeting comfort. As we ate, I watched the calm water stretch out endlessly before us, the clear daylight illuminating each of our faces. It had almost been a full day now, and there was a subtle sense of relief—a feeling that we were one day closer to our destination.

I chose not to continue that conversation with Kaviyani. Neither did I have the energy nor the desire, and besides, someone with a mindset like his wouldn't be convinced by any rational argument—definitely not in a situation like ours. In this environment, where even your food could be stolen without a hint of shame, perhaps Kaviyani's approach made sense. I had even experienced others offering me my own food, which they had stolen from my bag, as if it was nothing. It was almost laughable if it wasn't so infuriating.

We counted the days and nights impatiently, constantly asking the captain and his crew—who knew no English—how long it would take to reach our destination. One of the sailors kept holding up his fingers, signaling what we guessed to be two weeks, but the smuggler had assured us it would be 7-8 days at most. It became painfully clear to all of us that the smuggler had lied. He lied about the size of the boat, the number of people it could hold, the safety measures, and even the length of the journey. We felt foolish for not doing proper research, but back then, many of us didn't have the resources or the means to verify the information. Internet access was limited, and even if it wasn't, most of us didn't have the mindset to research this kind of journey in detail.

When we learned that we might be on the boat for far longer than expected, it was a crushing realization. We heard stories about boats that got lost at sea, and we knew that our only option was to trust the sailors and endure. Each sunrise became a beacon of hope. I watched every one of them, unable to sleep except when exhaustion overcame me.

Every new day meant I was still alive, and every night I looked at the bioluminescent glow of the water, wondering if this would be our last. I couldn't help but remember the little boy's innocent question: *Are we going to die tonight?* It echoed in my mind, especially during those nights when the storms raged, the boat tossed, and people screamed prayers, pleading for survival. There were life jackets and flotation tubes provided by the smuggler, but there weren't nearly enough for everyone.

Late at night, when the ocean was calm, everyone tried to keep quiet, whether they were asleep or awake. If people were chatting, it was in hushed whispers. We all needed that rare quiet—a signal that another day had passed and we were still here, still moving forward. During those times, I heard something strange: a man singing. At first, I thought it was someone from the family section, maybe Meherdad or one of the others. One day, when they came down to visit—which they often did—I asked Lili who was singing at night. To my surprise, she said, "No one. We thought it was one of you in the cabin or third level."

Everyone had heard it—a man singing the same song, night after night. It wasn't our imagination. But who could it be? It was puzzling, even a little unsettling. We wanted to ask the captain or the crew, but given their complete lack of English, it was almost impossible. We tried to use gestures, sign language, anything to communicate our question. When they finally understood, they just laughed at us. They insisted that they hadn't heard anything, but how could that be when over 80 of us had heard it clearly?

It's a question that has stayed with me ever since. I've spoken with others from the journey, and they too remember the singing—clear as day and always the same. We never got an answer, and it remains one of the strangest mysteries of that voyage. How could we all hear the same song, sung by an unseen man, when none of us could find the source? It still makes me shiver when I think about it.

It was impossible to say how many days had passed, but one midday, chaos erupted from the third level of the boat. People were screaming, shouting for help. Some of the boys quickly climbed up to see what had happened. Amid all the confusion, I heard them say that someone had fallen overboard. A wave of dread washed over me. Who had fallen into the ocean? I ran to the edge of the deck, trying to see who it was, and then I saw—it was Meherdad.

A chill ran through me, colder than anything the ocean could have thrown at me. For anyone else, falling into the ocean would have been terrifying, but for Meherdad, it was even worse. No one could afford to jump in after him—it wasn't just a matter of bravery; this was the ocean, a vast, powerful body of water with unforgiving waves. Meherdad was a big guy, and it would have been impossible for anyone to pull him out. The sailors threw a flotation tube towards him, urging him not to struggle too much and to conserve his energy.

I could barely see his face from the distance, but we all knew he was scared. Every second felt like an eternity as the waves carried him further from the boat. They had shut off the engine to prevent the boat from drifting away from him. I could feel my heart pounding in my ears, and when I looked at Lili—who was supposed to be his girlfriend—she was frozen, too terrified to say a word or make any move.

Someone must have noticed my face because they later told me I looked as pale as a ghost. All I could think about was what I would tell his parents if anything happened. Who would be brave enough to break such news to them? It felt as though time itself had stopped.

Finally, the sailors managed to throw a thick rope towards Meherdad. After several attempts, he caught it. Now, they had to pull him back in, which was no easy task. Not only was he heavy, but he was also exhausted, and there was a real chance he might lose his grip on the rope. Some of the boys, who had always resented his bossy attitude and envied him for his relationship with Lili, began muttering, "Leave him. He deserves this." Their bitterness spilled out—probably because Meherdad had been designated as the team leader and acted arrogantly about it.

I shot them a look filled with both anger and desperation, and they must have felt ashamed because they quickly fell silent. My whole body was shaking as if I had been plunged into ice-cold water. The memory of that young man who had died in Indonesia haunted me; the thought that we might lose Meherdad the same way was impossible .

After what felt like an eternity, they managed to pull him back onto the boat. Everyone cheered, except those who had earlier muttered curses—they still had something to say, but their voices were more subdued now. Meherdad climbed back on board with his head down, not saying a word, and no one expected him to either. The trauma of those moments must have weighed heavily on him.

The only positive outcome was that perhaps this experience might teach him some humility. His arrogance had always been noticeable, something that might have come from his athletic build, but maybe now he would learn to tone it down a bit. Once he was safe, I felt my legs give out, and I sank to my knees in the narrow passway. Someone—I'm not sure who—kindly handed me a glass of water, which, in our circumstances, felt like finding a treasure. Given the limited rationing, this small act of kindness was priceless.

A few hours later, the fear and tension of the incident seemed to dissipate. Everything returned to normal—people staring blankly at the ocean, counting the minutes, the boredom as heavy as the salty sea air. The routine resumed, but the unspoken tension remained. We had all come to realize how fragile our lives were in this unforgiving ocean.

Despite the tension and fear that hung over us, everyone shared the same goal: survival. We were now well past the first week, and still, the horizon offered no sign of land. I focused on the sunrise and sunset, taking each one as proof that we were still alive, but wondering each time if it might be our last.

During the daytime, we were told to stay seated as much as possible to avoid drawing attention from any ocean security patrols. Standing up made us too visible. We knew this area must not be under the control of the General or any informant they might have had, which heightened our vulnerability. If security forces spotted us, it would be over. Every time someone tried to stretch their legs by standing up, another person would shout at them to sit, leading to frequent arguments and, sometimes, fights. Among the singles, these fights were common—often serious enough that others had to intervene. It happened so many times that I stopped paying attention. The stress, the hunger, the thirst—all of it made everyone edgy, ready to snap at the slightest provocation.

There was nothing left for us to do but endure the endless monotony, hoping and praying that we could reach our destination before something irreversible happened.

Even though I often felt so down and tired, I preferred to stay in the cabin, keeping to myself. I would close my eyes, pretending to be unwell from seasickness, hoping it would discourage others from talking to me. When I did speak, it was mostly to Selma or her daughter Mina, who were always there with me. Sometimes, Rezi's mother would join us, and over time, she seemed softer, calmer, as if the weight of her earlier frustration had started to lift.

She opened up to me one day, explaining it was actually Rezi's decision to come this way. He had secretly converted to Christianity long ago, something that carried significant risk. For someone born Muslim, converting to another religion is considered a great, unforgivable sin. Despite being a devout Muslim herself, she hadn't objected to his conversion, though she tried, unsuccessfully, to convince him to change his mind. When she saw that Rezi was determined to leave, she decided to accompany him and also brought her daughter along.

It was hard to know whether to call it a deep sense of motherhood or selfishness. Many Iranian mothers, disappointed by their husbands' lack of love or support, transfer all their affection to their sons, which often leads to unintended consequences. She left her husband—perhaps for good reasons—but forced her daughter to come on this dangerous journey just to support Rezi, her favorite child.

The tension between the mother and daughter was palpable, with the daughter frequently showing her anger, even outright saying, "I hated coming here. You put my life at risk just because of your favorite son." The mother, on the other hand, had little to say in response. Anyone making this journey needed to be fully committed, or it would feel like a slow-motion disaster. The constant bickering between them narrated their reasons for making this trip, more so than any straightforward explanation could.

Luckily, most of their arguments were either contained in the cabin or on the upper level, away from the singles in another section. Their story stayed mostly between us, unlike others who had less private disputes.

Selma and Mina were entirely different. They had a beautiful relationship, one that was evident even in the small moments. Despite Mina being in her 30s, she often slept in her mother's arms, a gesture that spoke volumes about their bond. Mina once mentioned how surprised she was by Rezi's sister's behavior towards their mother, but I reminded her that we couldn't know all the details of someone else's life. Everyone had their own reasons and their own burdens.

Arya, meanwhile, couldn't stop vomiting. He could hardly keep anything down, and as the days dragged on, even the little food we had ran out. I gave him some hard, sour candies I had in my bag—the only thing he could keep down without throwing up. Even now, years later, he still calls me "Candy Auntie" whenever we cross paths. The last time I saw Arya was about seven years ago.

During the day, when the ocean was calmer, there was more time for everyone to mingle. Even late into the night, some stayed up, talking quietly, especially when those sitting on the upper level came down to escape the cold or the discomfort. Conversation was the only way to pass the time, but it would have been so much better with something to snack on. Unfortunately, most of us had long run out of snacks, and even the food provided by the smuggler was nearly gone.

Food became the one thing on everyone's mind. Conversations inevitably circled back to it, with people reminiscing about meals they once had, comparing what little they had left. It wasn't just hunger—it was the longing for the comfort of familiar tastes and the memory of normalcy. It was amazing how food became more than nourishment; it became a symbol of the life we were all desperately missing.

Chapter Thirteen

The third time on this journey, Selma and Mina were both familiar with what it meant to be in a boat like this, crossing such dangerous waters. I had been with them on their second attempt, and it was clear that experience didn't always make it easier. Selma was hopeful that once she reached Australia, she could rely on her son and a wide network of friends and family already there to help them start over. Despite their experience, Mina was still so scared. One night, in the cabin, she started crying uncontrollably, and I tried to comfort her, though I knew my words might not change much.

She finally blurted out something that made me laugh, and, to my surprise, she started laughing at her own silly thoughts too. She said, "I'm having my period. If we drown, I'm going to be the first one the sharks come for!" I laughed and told her, "I think my meat would be tastier for the sharks—I'm fairer-skinned."

Our laughter was contagious, and soon everyone in the cabin, even those feeling grim, started laughing. Even the man with his wife and children, who had been sleeping in the cabin after all those arguments with people in the upper level, cracked a smile. Thankfully, no one had thrown him overboard, but they had certainly made it clear he was no longer welcome up there.

It felt good to have a moment of laughter. Sara, Kaviyani's wife, joined in the joking, saying, "No sharks are going to eat us—they'll eat the kids first. They have the most tender meat." The words slipped out, and her face changed as soon as she realized what she had said. Kaviyani gave her a sharp look, and the humor of the situation was suddenly overshadowed by its darkness. It was a bitter joke, one that left us all with heavy hearts, thinking about those innocent children who were asleep beside her.

The cabin fell silent. I looked at those two young kids—blissfully unaware of what was happening—and felt the deep sadness that Sara must have felt, trapped in a situation like this with a dominating, bullying husband who barely let her speak. She had been too young when she married him, and coming from a strict, traditional family, she knew nothing but compliance. That, sadly, was her version of normal.

Azar, on the other hand, was different. She had a strong sense of independence and often clashed with Kaviyani. She wasn't afraid to speak her mind, even if it meant standing up against his unfair behavior. She frequently took Sara's side, and they, along with Sherri and Reza, formed a close-knit group, planning enthusiastically what they would do once they landed safely in Australia. There was an innocence in their dreams—a kind of unspoiled hope that was comforting to see. It was good they hadn't let fear or doubt take away their hope. It reminded me of the dreams we had in our younger years, full of ambition but unaware of the harsh realities that awaited us.

I was probably the only one among them who had experienced life in a Western country. I knew how different the reality would be from their dreams—how the challenges of settling down, finding jobs, and adapting would shatter their idealistic visions. When the hardships of migration hit, it wouldn't be easy to keep that hope alive. Still, who was I to take that from them? We all needed our dreams.

We were nearing the end of our journey, at least according to what we had been told. The water supply was nearly gone, and our daily ration had already been reduced. Food, if anyone still had any, was incredibly scarce, and any sharing was unlikely at this stage. Selma and Mina, being more experienced, had stocked up a large bag of food that they kept hidden from everyone. Late at night, when others were asleep, they would quietly take it out and eat. I saw it happen many times during my sleepless hours, and it was heartbreaking—to feel they needed to hide their own food. They were just trying to survive, but the secrecy added another layer of despair.

Mina had grown close to one of the boys in charge of food distribution. She'd sometimes sneak him a portion of their food, and in return, he'd give her a bit more water. Food was everything at that point, and even though they had the right to keep what was theirs, others were watching, hoping for a shred of kindness. One day, Lili, who was clearly suffering from stomach pain, hinted to Mina about her discomfort, expecting a small offering. Mina, however, just handed her some painkillers. Lili shot me a look that seemed to say, "See what I got for all that hope."

The dry noodles provided by the smuggler had to be eaten uncooked because there wasn't enough water to boil them. We chewed on those hard, tasteless noodles like they were some kind of luxury snack. Even years later, just the sight of those noodles still makes me feel sick. But back then, chewing those dry noodles felt like indulging in a five-star meal. I could tell I had lost a lot of weight—my pants kept slipping down, and I had to tie them with a piece of rope I found on the deck. Everyone was in a similar state: pale, weakened, and gaunt, our lips cracked from dehydration.

The captain and his crew had their own food supply, which nobody dared to ask for. We all knew how important it was for them to stay strong and healthy, and their well-being was probably more crucial to us than our own. The crew had grown a little friendlier, especially one older sailor who always treated us with a surprising amount of care and respect. He must have been illiterate, from a lower social class, but there was something genuine about him that made us all like him. In our vulnerable state, it was easy to either love or hate intensely. Meherdad and Lili's sudden connection, Mina's dealings with the boy for extra water—emotions were raw and immediate.

In such a confined space, there was no hiding our affections or our frustrations. The old sailor earned our affection just by being kind, while Kaviyani, with his unending anger, garnered the opposite. Despite his children, I could find no empathy for him. His constant need to assert his power was exhausting. Even if his intentions were to protect his family, he went about it in the worst possible way.

These days felt like an eternity. Every night, I would watch the dark waves and wonder if we would see the next sunrise. For all our planning and calculating, survival here was anything but certain.

One night, when we were all supposed to be sleeping—or at least trying to close our eyes—my patience finally ran out. Kaviyani was lying down, sprawled out as wide as he could, and I was sure he was doing it on purpose. We were all trying so hard to take up as little space as possible, given how cramped our situation was. I asked him to pull himself together, but instead, he spread out even more. My anger boiled over, and I yelled at him with a loud voice, "Do you think you're lying in front of a TV in your own home?"

My shout seemed to awaken something in everyone else too. They began to yell at him, making it clear that this wasn't the time or place for selfishness. He finally put himself together, and the pressure from all of us seemed to get through to him. Some people even talked about reporting his behavior once we got to the detention center. I had heard rumors about the detention centers—that the authorities kept track of behavior, and any report of bad conduct could lead to a darker situation, perhaps making it harder to be released. Whether it was true or not, it seemed like it was something that worried people. I later found out that Kaviyani and his family were, indeed, held in detention longer than any other family group—almost a year.

Most of the single passengers faded from my memory, as they were on a different level of the boat and not easy to see. Occasionally, someone would recognize me on the street, calling out, "Auntie, you were with us on the boat!" And though they would greet me warmly, I couldn't always remember their faces. One day, early on in our journey, the food distribution team served us coffee. I had helped pass around plastic cups filled with hot coffee, giving everyone a small bit of comfort. Years later, while in Sydney on business, a young man, now in his thirties, approached me. He spoke softly, looking at me with gratitude, "I'll never forget the day you handed me that hot cup of coffee. It saved my body and soul."

I felt embarrassed by his appreciation because, back then, I had merely been doing a simple task. His words brought tears to my eyes. I wondered if I should have been more caring during those days. Maybe my self-preserving neutrality was worse than the people who yelled, swore, or fought. Even now, I'm not sure which reaction was better, and I can't say for sure that I would do any better if faced with the same situation again.

It was almost nine days since we'd set sail, and still, there was no land in sight—only the ocean stretching endlessly around us. People were growing more restless. The slightest excuse could spark a fight—verbal clashes were more common among the family group, while the singles often fought physically. These fights sometimes got so intense that we all had to intervene, pulling people apart. The last thing we needed was someone getting badly hurt, but by then, Arya, who had been vomiting since the start, seemed practically injured just from his weakened state.

On the tenth day, he began vomiting blood, and we were terrified. We forced him to drink water each day, but one time, as I was coaxing him to drink, I saw tears streaming down his face. He looked so quiet and desperate, and it was one of the saddest moments I experienced during those days.

On the tenth day, the pain throughout my body was unbearable. I hadn't had even one proper night's sleep, which was no surprise given our conditions. My head throbbed, and my injured knee ached constantly. I couldn't stand it anymore, so I decided to take one of the sleeping pills I had with me. The least it could do was help me forget everything for a few hours.

After the sun had set, I swallowed a pill and sat to have a chat with Selma, waiting for it to take effect. Selma was wise and had many stories to share. She told me that she and Mina had come here with Mina's husband. They were newly married, but Mina's husband had a son from a previous marriage, and they couldn't get along. So, they separated, and he decided to take the journey separately, joining another group. Selma and Mina had been in Indonesia for a long time, waiting for their chance. This was their third attempt, just like me, and each previous time, something had gone wrong. When they ran out of money, the smuggler had provided for their basic needs while they waited.

Selma's son and his wife had traveled the same route months before and were now settled in Melbourne. She came from a tribe, many members of which were already in Australia, and she had faith that they would help her. Her husband and another daughter were still back home—her husband was too sick to make this journey. She was a few years younger than me, but her wisdom and some of the advice she gave me during our conversation that night are things I still hold onto. Mina, though not a child, was highly dependent on her mother and couldn't understand Razi's sister's attitude toward her mother. Respect for parents seemed to be like a Bible verse for Mina, and she often commented on how she couldn't fathom Gelareh's defiance.

Soon, the sleeping pill took effect, and I fell into a deep sleep. I had been hoping for sweet dreams instead of the nightmares that had haunted me recently, ones that had even made me scream out loud during naps, waking others in the cabin. It was still late at night when I was abruptly awakened by a commotion—everyone was making noise, and all the lights were on. Normally, the captain was careful not to leave the lights on to avoid attracting unwanted attention from the ocean's patrols, and there had even been stories about pirates. Though I never believed the pirate stories, I knew enough not to dismiss people's fears entirely.

Mina's eyes were wide with fear as she told me that a fast boat had arrived and the captain had left. Before leaving, he told everyone that we were now in Australian waters and that the navy would soon come to get us. He claimed he had to leave before they arrived. But all we could see around us was water, and no one knew whether to trust his words. It felt like he had abandoned us in the middle of the ocean. But if he intended to betray us, why would he have sailed us this far? Besides, the two crew members were still with us.

The captain had left, and the confusion was overwhelming. People were shouting, trying to come up with a solution. Eventually, we decided to wait until morning. Then, one man mentioned that he had a special satellite phone, one that could make calls from anywhere. He also said he had the number for the Australian maritime security guard. We could call them when the sun came up and explain our situation—they would find us, even if we didn't know our exact location.

I wanted to ask why he had kept this phone a secret, but from the way others reacted, I understood why. Apparently, having such a phone was forbidden—it could be seen as a tool for spying, and once we called the navy, we would have to throw it into the ocean to avoid arrest. Whether this was true or just another story, I wasn't sure. But I clung to the hope that maybe, finally, we had a way to survive.

After spending almost ten nights in the ocean, this was by far the hardest night for all of us—none of us could wait until morning. Fortunately, it wasn't a stormy night. I sat on the passageway, where there were now only a few barrels left, making it easier for people to sit or pass. I watched the waves, illuminated by the glow of the bioluminescent aquatic life, thinking to myself: was it finally time to say goodbye to our aquatic friends or time for our exhausted, defeated bodies to feed them?

At dawn, two people were chosen to make the call, and to my surprise, I was one of them. Perhaps they trusted me more or relied on my better English skills; I wasn't sure what earned me the honor. The man with the phone asked me to come with him to the third level, believing it might have better reception from the higher vantage point. He didn't give me the number—he dialed it himself. The phone was huge, looking like one of those early versions of mobile phones, only even larger. My hands were shaking, barely able to hold it steady, and the silence around us was thick. Not even the slightest noise could be heard from anyone.

The first beep, then the second, and by the third ring, someone answered, their voice heavy with a strong accent. I told him that we were 81 people, with children, and we had a man in poor health (Arya, who was vomiting blood). I struggled to hear him at first, but after repeating himself a few times, I caught what he said. "Do you know where you are?" he asked.

"No, we have no idea," I replied. "We don't have the equipment to determine our location."

"Stay where you are," he instructed. "We will find you soon."

His voice sounded clear, but I still had trouble hearing him. That's when I realized—my hearing was damaged. One ear seemed almost deaf, and the other was weak. Perhaps it was the constant noise of the ocean or the stress that numbed my senses, but up until that moment, I hadn't fully noticed.

With my voice trembling, I asked him, "Do you promise to come for us? Please, for the sake of these children, come. Don't let us die out here." I was crying as I said this, and a strange feeling of closeness to this stranger washed over me. It felt as if he was a loved one, a family member, someone whose shoulder I could rest my head on and ask for mercy. He repeated, "I assure you, we will come for you in two hours."

I hung up and told everyone what he had said. Everyone was crying—tears of hope, of relief. I ran to Arya, who lay on the floor, his face against it, crying silently. He said, "If I die here, my father will also die of sorrow." I lifted his head and said, "Don't cry; we are not going to die. They are coming for us."

Back in the cabin, I hugged Selma and Mina tightly. They had big smiles on their faces and tears on their cheeks. Everyone, with their tired and devastated appearances, was getting ready for the navy to come. For the first time in a long time, I witnessed the most beautiful sunrise. The sky seemed to promise that life was going to go on. People hugged whoever was next to them, including Kaviyani, whom nobody had liked before. Even he had a big smile and tears in his eyes, proving that underneath all his gruffness, he was simply a desperate father. No one talked about death anymore.

But as midday approached and the navy had not yet arrived, a sense of unease began to creep back in. If they didn't show up soon, all the hope and happiness we'd experienced would vanish like bubbles on the waves. People started asking me to call again, and there was no disagreeing with them. Everyone was far too tired and hopeless to accept any logic that suggested waiting. I went with the man and the big phone to the third level to make another call. Suddenly, we heard a plane—a boy screamed in excitement, "Look, there's a plane above us!"

We all started screaming, waving our hands, our faces alight with joy. We had heard before that when the navy locates your boat, they first send a plane to find you. Whatever the reason was—to verify our position or something else—it didn't matter. The plane was a sign of salvation. The mother with the kids stood beside me, and so did Meherdad. I told him, "Pick up the kids so they can see we have children with us." The happiness and relief in that moment were incomparable to anything else we had ever experienced.

Now, we were sure that rescue was near, and we wouldn't have to wait much longer. The boat remained still—we didn't dare move it since the captain had left.

Chapter Fourteen

The atmosphere on board of the boat had quickly shifted from elation to despair. Just moments ago, we had been filled with hope, cheering as the navy soldiers broke into our boat, their handsome figures seeming like angels sent to save us. Their presence, the loud noise of their arrival, and the sight of their uniforms were the most beautiful things we'd seen in so long. But now, they were gone, and that feeling of safety vanished as quickly as it had arrived.

The navy soldiers had come in, assessed our condition, asked a few questions, and then instructed us on what would happen next. They'd even taken time to give us numbers, and I was assigned KEY059. I'd laughed nervously, wondering what destiny this number would bring into the next chapter of my life. But despite the registration and assurances, they wouldn't take us onto their ship. Instead, they told us to follow them with our own boat, and soon they were gone, as if the hope of rescue had never really existed.

In the wake of their departure, chaos erupted. Everyone had an opinion—ideas and theories that they'd heard from others, from rumors, from passengers who'd been through similar journeys. Some believed the navy soldiers had lied to us, others thought they were never going to come back. The accusations flew like arrows, and I found myself at the center of them all. I tried to calm everyone, explaining that the navy had their rules, and that they wouldn't abandon us after making contact. I tried to assure them that they would fulfill their duty, but most people were too scared to believe it. One man accused me, tears streaming down his face, "Ms. Zartabi, you ruined our lives. We are going to die here, and it's your fault."

It was heartbreaking, and I felt a chill running through my entire body. I had been doing my best to communicate with the navy. It wasn't about my English skills—it was about laws, about processes that had to be followed. But nobody wanted to hear my explanations. Some of the young men even blamed me for not crying and begging enough, as if showing more emotion could have changed the outcome. I could feel their anger intensifying, the desperation pushing them to find someone to blame, someone to lash out at in their moment of fear.

Meherdad, Lili, and the others from the family group were up on the first level, staying away from the turmoil down below. I was all alone, surrounded by angry voices. The athletic young man from my previous boat experience—the one who'd always treated me with politeness and respect—was sobbing uncontrollably, and it broke my heart even more. I could hear him repeating, "We're going to die, and it's her fault."

The accusations kept coming, and they hurt more than any physical pain I'd ever felt. I sat down, my head in my hands, feeling the weight of everyone's fear and blame bearing down on me. I was exhausted, worn out, and scared. My hope that the navy would come back was the only thing keeping me together. I knew that if they didn't, if something went wrong, the anger around me could turn violent.

One of the boys decided he would start the engine and try to move the boat, to follow the navy's instructions. He was trying to do what the soldiers had said, but almost immediately, the others shouted at him, telling him to stop, to sit down, that he was making a mistake. He hesitated, then turned the engine off, not wanting to go against the collective fear and anger of the group.

I tried one last time to appeal to them. "Please, trust the navy," I said, my voice cracking from exhaustion. "They have found us. They have a duty, and they will fulfill it. We need to be patient." But my words fell on deaf ears. All I saw in their eyes was a mix of fear and resentment.

I slumped down, feeling helpless and utterly alone. If the navy didn't return soon, I genuinely didn't know what would happen. Would the crowd turn on me completely? Would their desperation lead them to violence, to finding an outlet for all the frustration they'd been harboring for days? I buried my face in my hands, whispering a silent prayer that they would come back in time, that they wouldn't abandon us to the darkness of this ocean and the despair in our hearts.

The moment the navy soldiers returned felt like salvation itself. I watched them arrive, my heart pounding as they approached our broken boat. For a brief moment, their faces were like those of guardian angels, and I felt a rush of relief that was almost overwhelming. One of the soldiers turned to me, asking why we weren't following them as instructed. But I was exhausted, my head aching from the stress and the harsh accusations that had been thrown at me.

I stepped aside, gesturing to the other man who had some knowledge of English. I pointed at him and said, "Let him handle it," and then moved to sit with the rest of the family members. I couldn't bear to face more misunderstandings or do anything that might provoke more blame. As I slumped down, I noticed the shift in the expressions around me— shame mixed with relief. Their faces were now softened, and they looked at me differently, as if they realized their mistake. But it was too late; their cold shoulders had already made these two hours feel like two eternities.

The other man attempted to speak to the navy soldiers, his broken English sounding hesitant. I could see that he was struggling. Every now and then, he came over to me, asking for clarification about what the soldiers were saying. I whispered the answers to him, helping him as best as I could, though it felt ironic that I was now guiding the person they had replaced me with. I was still struggling to hear properly, so he had to lean in close, and I felt a pang of awkwardness mixed with resignation. The boys—perhaps because they were getting tired of his poor translation or because they felt I could do it better—started insisting that I take over. But I refused, not out of spite, but because the headache I had was unbearable. The constant pressure was wearing me down.

Selma, with her big smile, asked jokingly, "Are you spoiling yourself?" I gave her a hug, smiling back, and said, "Yes." We both laughed; it was a moment of joy, a shared understanding. I wanted to show her that I was still happy despite everything, despite the hurtful words and the blame I'd carried. I knew it was important to hold on to these positive moments. I told myself that this was my first lesson in this new country—if I was going to start a new life here, I had to plan carefully, to be cautious about who I helped. But I knew myself too well. Deep down, I was a terrible student when it came to such lessons. I couldn't help but give in to my instinct to help, no matter what.

After some time, the soldiers began their task of transferring us in groups to the big navy ship. They had promised to take the families first, and while it took longer than expected, seeing that massive ship so close, with all its lights shining on the water, was something beyond any of our dreams. We all stared at it, mesmerized by its grand appearance. I didn't know how much time had passed since the boat had stopped moving. None of us had watches, and time itself had lost its meaning in the ocean. But now, waiting to board the ship felt like waiting to be born again. There was laughter, hope, and conversations about the bright future awaiting us on land.

All the boys from the first level had come down and joined the rest of us, scattered across the second and third levels, blending in with the family group. I sat on the passway, resting as much as I could. One of the boys sitting near me asked,

"I've had a question for you all this time:

Why would a woman your age take such a risk?"

His curiosity was genuine, and I knew this question had probably crossed the minds of many people on the boat. In our culture, it was uncommon for a woman my age to embark on something so dangerous, especially in her fifties. I smiled mysteriously, feeling a sense of victory, and replied,

"Who knows? Maybe at this age, I can do better than all the young people here."

Selma and Mina burst into laughter, and soon, the joyful sound spread among the others. It was the laughter of people who had survived, who had seen death and lived to tell the story. Even Kaviyani, who had always carried that gruff, unapproachable demeanor, had a smile on his face, his eyes wet with tears. It seemed as though, for the first time in a long while, we could let our guard down and feel happiness without fear. It wasn't the end yet, but it was the beginning of something new—something we had all dared to dream about in our darkest moments.

I looked out at the ocean, at the magnificent ship that promised safety, and for the first time, I believed we were truly going to make it. Whatever lay ahead, whether it was in Darwin or elsewhere, at least it wouldn't be here, stranded in the middle of nowhere, with only our desperation to keep us company. It was the promise of land, of a new chapter, and no matter how hard it was, we were ready to face it. We had already survived the impossible, and we were about to begin again.

I don't know how long it took, but I guess it was midnight when they began taking family groups in those small, fast boats, driving them to the big ship. They took Kaviyani, his wife, and their kids first. The interpreter was with them too—maybe in case they needed his help. Then it was Selma and Mina. After that, it was my turn. Each trip took less than 20 minutes for the boat to return for the next person or group. Now, finally, it was my turn.

I don't know why we didn't all get into the small boat together, though it seemed strong and firm. Perhaps it was a safety measure. But for us, traveling across the ocean with 81 people in a medium-sized fishing boat, talking about safety measures didn't make much sense. When it was my turn, I had to walk over a narrow railing to jump onto the small boat. Just like when I boarded the boat at midnight, getting on that fast boat wasn't easy either. I had to make a small jump.

One of the soldiers reached out his hand to help me, but when the time came to jump, I missed my step and couldn't grab his hand. My body, like everyone else's, was stiff and dry from days without much movement. I nearly fell into the water, but the soldier grabbed my hand just in time, pulling me back when half of my body was already dangling over the edge. The others were watching, and when each of us boarded safely, they cheered. But when I almost fell, they all screamed in fear.

Finally, I made it into the small boat. Its lights were on, not bright enough to illuminate the ocean, but enough to see the water just ahead of us and the faces around me. Just a glance at the large ship—sitting there, so powerful and grand—was enough to warm our souls and fill us with a sense of safety.

Then the boat turned away from the ship, which wasn't the same move it made when it took others before me. I couldn't believe I had survived, and stupidly, I thought they might be taking me to throw me into the water because I was older than everyone else and might be seen as useless, a burden. These foolish thoughts rushed through my mind in a second, born out of desperation—like when Mina was afraid that if sharks attacked, she would be eaten first because she was on her period. Soon enough, the boat took its path toward the big ship again.

I looked back and waved to my beloved nephew, Meherdad. He was standing next to Lili, a big smile on his face. He waved back, as if saying, "We did it!" That was the last time I saw him, even up until today. Later, Meherdad and the others were transferred to another ship and we were split into separate groups.

I had imagined that this makeshift aunt-nephew relationship would last forever—that once we were all safe, we would sit, talk, eat, and laugh about all the difficult moments. But the nephew I borrowed out of necessity had to be "returned," as if his role for me, for filling the void of a family member, had ended. It wasn't for me—I still miss him after all these years.

A few weeks after we were released into the community, he called me late one night to say our family relationship was over, and he no longer wished to stay in contact. Wherever he is, whatever he does, he is always in my heart as my nephew. I wish him the best, not just him but all those with whom I shared these moments of being caught between life and death.

They are always in my mind, and most importantly, in my heart. Whether I see them again or not, we shared the most vital moments of our lives. I experienced death and rebirth with them—something I have never experienced with anyone else, not even the most important people in my life—and I will honor that for the rest of my days.

It took about 7 to 10 minutes for the fast boat to take me to the big ship. Though I had seen it from a distance, its greatness and the sense of glory it exuded, with all those lights, the huge deck, and all the soldiers, was beyond my imagination. I was so worn out, feeling small and weak from everything I had been through. To my tired, hopeless eyes, it seemed even more spectacular and vast—especially for a woman who had resigned herself to dying just the night before.

A tall, young, handsome man in uniform was waiting for me at the stairs. I got out of the boat with the help of another soldier, and the young man offered me his hand. It felt as though I had adopted all the power and grandeur of that ship in an instant. I suddenly felt an extra surge of strength fill me, born from the safety of the moment. I didn't take the young soldier's hand, even though it was offered so kindly.

Maybe, from the very first moment of stepping on board, I wanted to shout out that although I wasn't as young as the others, I wasn't as needy as my age might suggest. In my culture, it's an ingrained belief that age means decline, that usefulness has ended. And even though I've often rejected that belief, it's been whispered into my ear enough times that maybe, on some level, I've internalized it.

The young soldier led me to a corner of the deck where the lights were off. There, I saw Kaviyani, his wife, and their children, along with Selma, Mina, and the young man who had been translating—all asleep on the floor. They lay quietly on mattresses, each with a blanket. A blanket! Oh, the luxurious feeling of having a blanket on them. Even before I put one on, the sight of it made me feel warm. There were no pillows, but the mat beneath them was more than we had dared hope for.

They were only a few hours ahead of me in this seven-star ship deck "hotel" and everyone was in a deep sleep. The children were curled up in their mother's arms, with their father beside them. He, too, was sleeping deeply, finally at peace, knowing his family was safe. Nobody in the boat liked him much; his defensiveness was often unnecessary. But at that moment, he seemed like a lion protecting his family—a father lion with a mother lion and two cubs. His attitude may not have been acceptable, but had anything in this journey been normal or acceptable? That was the only way he knew to mask his fear and protect his family. From that perspective, he was respectable, selfless for their sake. Each one of us had our share of unacceptable attitudes during this journey, and in most cases, we had a right to it—we didn't have time for politeness.

Unlike when we were on the boat, no one was pretending to be asleep now—they were truly in a deep sleep. We used to pretend to be asleep because it was the only way to have a sense of privacy, a survival tactic. I almost threw myself onto that cool mat, which seemed to be kindly waiting for me. When I lay down, I saw Mina's eyes open, and she gave me a big smile with a mischievous sparkle in her eyes, still nestled in her mother's arms. That was the last thing I saw before I, too, fell into a deep sleep. We didn't exchange any words, but we both understood the meaning behind her smile and the gleam in her eyes. It was a smile that spoke of relief, a shared secret that we had made it.

It was the most peaceful and relaxing sleep I had ever had in my life, with no fear of death or of getting lost helplessly in the ocean. We had all come back to life from the brink of death, and none of us would take life for granted again—I was sure of it. I don't think I have ever had such a sleep since that night, not even once. There was a peace then that I have never felt again, not even when in my own bed at home. I missed the twilight we had witnessed every day from the boat—it would have been an even better view from the deck of the ship.

I woke up to the sound of soldiers cleaning the deck, dragging something like a large mop across the floor. The friction made a strangely beautiful sound, waking me gently. Others woke up one by one: the children first, then their parents, then the young man and Selma. Mina was the last to wake up. The soldier was cleaning up the mess from our dirty clothes and the filthy water that had dripped from us the night before. I felt a bit embarrassed at how dirty and messy we all were.

I took a better look at everyone's faces in the daylight. A different glow colored them now—a joy touched by the flavor of freedom. It was something so special that even the children understood the difference between then and now. We had survived; the danger that had trapped us was behind us.

The first thing on everyone's mind was how hungry we were. I asked the soldier if we could eat something, especially for the kids. He called another man, who brought a tray with small packets of long-life milk and slices of chocolate cake for each of us. He then said, "The Captain will join you later, and you will be served breakfast with him."

Oh, what a luxury! So this wasn't our breakfast? He smiled and said, "No, this is just a snack before the main breakfast." We looked at each other, our faces filled with disbelief. Oh, God, how cool and tasty that milk and cake were! I could feel every crumb of the cake and every sip of the cool milk with my entire soul.

We were all talking about what might come next for us. The young man began telling us stories about the detention centers that he had heard from friends who had been through the same experience in the past. He continued, saying we were still lucky, having only been at sea for 11 days. Some people he knew had gotten lost and wandered the ocean for a month with no food or water. Although we had very little water and almost no food, compared to what he described, our situation had been better.

I couldn't imagine what a detention center would be like, as I had never experienced anything like it. Just hearing the name made me think it couldn't possibly be the kind of heaven this man was describing. Selma confirmed parts of what he said, explaining that many of her in-laws had made this journey over the past 10 years, and her son had done so a few months ago. She said most of what the young man said was correct and even added that the detention center's facilities were luxurious.

I listened quietly, as did Kaviyani and his family, but honestly, it was hard for me to believe everything they said. Maybe the part about how they take care of children was true, but they painted a picture of heaven for us. They continued, saying that only the detention center in Darwin had such good facilities. The ones on Christmas Island, where most asylum seekers landed, were not as good.

It was still a nice place with all the required facilities to be comfortable, but Darwin was truly a hotel for all asylum seekers. For the first time during this journey, someone used the term "asylum seeker" to describe us. How could I ever forget that this is what defines my identity now? It started the moment they called me by a number—KEY059. That was my name, and I had no idea how long it would be my identity.

I went through all of this just to gain the freedom I deserve as a human being, but now I am unsure if I've lost my identity in the process too. I am officially an asylum seeker, but I don't know what that title means for my life. I came for freedom and safety—will this simple word provide me what I came for, or will I just be a number for the rest of my life? It's too late to worry about these things now. All I can do is wait and see what comes next.

Soon, a man with a big pot in his hands, followed by a few navy soldiers, walked toward us. He sat down on the mat, his face humble and cheerful. "I am the captain of this ship," he said, "and I brought your breakfast. I'll have breakfast with you." His gentle and respectful attitude toward us felt like a promise of how others might treat us as asylum seekers.

But I knew it was too soon, and perhaps naive, to judge our future based on the kindness of just one person. These were the first hours of our new experience as asylum seekers, and I had heard many stories—both overt and subtle—of how asylum seekers face discrimination. Now, we were in their hands, and a new challenge had begun. I had to acknowledge the reality: this was their home, and I had barged in uninvited. All I could do was hope that they would treat us fairly.

The captain distributed what they called porridge in small bowls among us and began asking about our journey. I supposed he already knew how it must have been—everyone knows the dangers of traveling the ocean on a makeshift raft, especially with so many people. He seemed genuinely sympathetic and explained, "Unfortunately, we can't accommodate you in cabins, so you must stay on the deck until we arrive in Darwin tomorrow. But we will organize a shed for you and provide a portable toilet and other essentials. You'll be served food and can walk around, but just within your designated area. You can't move around the rest of the ship as it's against the law."

I replied, "We are more than happy with these conditions. It's far better than the fear of dying in the ocean or getting lost." He continued to give us more information about our arrival in Darwin and what we could expect.

Despite having been hungry for so long and dreaming of food, none of us could eat what they called porridge. I didn't even know what it was until later. When I learned about a typical Aussie breakfast, I was relieved it wasn't Vegemite—because even though we managed a few spoonful of porridge out of politeness, I don't think I could have done the same with Vegemite. As I returned the bowls, I told the captain, "Our stomachs and appetites have shrunk from not eating for so long. That's all we can manage for now." He seemed to understand, and they left us to rest.

The young man, with a teasing smile, said, "That's the kind of food you're going to get in Australia." I shot back, "Don't worry, we'll give them the real taste of food with our cuisine in the future," and everyone burst out laughing. Oh, real laughter—not a bitter smile. How beautiful it was, that feeling of laughter, with butterflies in your stomach and joy in every cell.

The rest of the day passed as we planned for the future, with everyone eagerly sharing their dreams. It might not be a sure home yet, but it doesn't hurt to dream. Today, it might feel uncertain to call it home, but who knows what the future will bring? Whatever it is, I believe it will be as bright as the sunshine on this deck.

Lunch was much better—canned tuna with rice and vegetables. I must say, we all attacked the plate, and it vanished in less than five minutes. Oh, what a wonderful feeling it was to have a full stomach again. I had almost forgotten these simple joys. It made me remember all the wastefulness of my past life—leaving the tap running for too long when others were dying for just a drop of water or even a little bit of food. But please, don't blame us for not finishing our porridge bowls earlier; it was our first time facing Aussie food, and porridge just wasn't to our liking. Were we being too picky? I don't know, but it just didn't work for us that day.

By the afternoon, they had set up a shed over us, just in time, as the rain and storm started. Sitting out in the storm wasn't easy, but the shed made it bearable. Besides, it was far better compared to when we were in the boat during the rains and storms.

When the storm, with its heavy rain, finally ended, we were given the chance to walk around, though not far from our designated area. I was amazed at how fast this ship moved—oh my God, how quickly it sailed! I thought about how it had already taken us almost two days on this fast ship; if we had stayed on that little raft, how long would it have taken us to reach anywhere—if we ever made it at all?

The boat had broken just at the right time when the ship was nearby, and even they couldn't fix it. What if it had happened earlier, before they reached us? Considering the first time we tried boarding, it would have surely been the end for us, just as it had been for so many others before.

Even thinking about that possibility was terrifying. Maybe God spared our lives for the sake of those two little kids. But then, many others who drowned also had children with them. It's a matter of destiny, luck, or whatever it is. Selfishly, I was just happy it didn't happen to us. You take your life in your hands—and even worse, your children's lives—and offer them to the ocean, which then decides whether to accept or reject you. That rejection, the ocean sparing us, was the most wonderful rejection anyone could ever hope for.

All our blankets and mats were wet from the storm. I asked for dry blankets and mats, feeling a bit embarrassed. I wondered if I should even expect any more favors. The young man insisted it was nonsense to feel embarrassed to ask for what we needed; the soldiers were just doing their job, after all. But for me, the fact that I was here in what felt like an unaccepted form of migration was hard to shake. I don't know if it was because of all I had heard about how asylum seekers are treated or if it was simply the way I was brought up—not to expect more than I was given. It was difficult for me to ask for any extra services.

The young man was only with us initially to help with interpreting, but as soon as we arrived on the ship, he seemed to pass that responsibility to me. I didn't mind, of course. Later, he was transferred to a separate detention center, but it seemed like he had already forgotten his role or maybe didn't have enough confidence in his language skills when I was around. For whatever reason, I didn't mind continuing to help with interpreting at all.

Only one night away from total care. Yes, safety was definitely there—at least far more than we'd had so far. But freedom? I wasn't sure yet. It depended on their interpretation of the freedom they wanted to grant us. In the eyes of the officials and the government back home, I was considered "free" too, yet I wasn't even allowed to choose my own clothing style or decide what to read or write. Their interpretation of freedom was entirely wrong.

Whatever awaits me, I know I chose it by my own will. Even just thinking about choosing my own lifestyle and the destiny waiting for me fills me with a joy beyond anything else. Before, I wasn't truly a human being—I was just a woman, and in reality, that meant being considered nobody. So many unreasonable rules had been imposed on women and even now in this era, they persist. It may seem impossible to those who have always lived with the freedom to choose their path, but it is the reality for women in the Middle East.

How beautiful the sunset was from the ship's deck. It was the same sun I had seen thousands of times, even from the boat, but this sunset wasn't just a sunset—it was the sunrise of my new life. I can't say the same about the actual sunrise, because in the two days aboard the ship, I hadn't seen it. I was too exhausted, passed out in deep sleep, but the next sunrise was just around the corner.

And finally, that next sunrise came, on July 7th, 2013, at twilight, as we landed in Darwin. I asked the date from one of the navy soldiers, and I told myself, "Remember this day for the rest of your life." I saw seagulls flying above us, their calls a symphony of joy, happiness, safety, welcome, and perhaps freedom. Our dirty faces, our worn, muddy, and smelly clothes, were all covered by happy smiles.

I could even sense that our happiness had spread to the navy soldiers as they looked at us. Some of them smiled at us, while others, like one of the women among them—who had been cold and distant when we boarded—still had the same expression. But that was okay. Even for those who weren't happy about our presence, I now had time to prove myself. I promised I would repay the kindness they showed me, doing my best to contribute to this country's prosperity, and I would change their minds. Instead of resentment, I offered them my smile.

We both knew what that smile meant: Yes, I made it. I was safe, alive, and here. This was the reward for what I had fought for, and I would make that reward worth it with my hard work, resilience, and loyalty.

We got help getting off the ship, and the moment my feet touched the ground, I bowed and sat on the earth, kissing it—just as I had promised to do while we were on the boat. I had spoken about this with Selma, and now, seeing her in front of me, she reminded me of my words. I said aloud, "Yes," and she did the same. We both laughed loudly, unashamed of our laughter, because everyone around us knew we had every right to laugh—we had come back from hell.

Everything around me was so overwhelming that I didn't hear a woman speaking to me at first. Or maybe it was because of my ears, which had been having trouble since we were on the boat. She repeated herself, louder and closer now. "If you have any money or jewelry with you, you must give it to me now. It will be returned to you when you are released from the detention center," she said. I reached into my bra, where I had a secret pocket for my money. She raised her hand and said again, louder, "Your jewelry." My jewelry? I hadn't even realized I still had my wedding ring and earrings on me. I handed them over and walked toward a waiting van.

Where were they taking us? I didn't know, and I didn't care. Wherever it was, it was safe. I was sure this was my first step toward the new chapter of my life, and I promised myself that I would make every other chapter worthy of all I had been through. I owed it to those who lost their lives in the ocean, to create for myself what they could not. I owed it to my own being, dignity and self-respect.

I sat in the van, feeling even a bit sorry for the seat, given my dirty clothes. I repeated to myself, "It's July 7th, 2013. The sun is almost in the sky now." The fatal experience that began in that *spot* has led you to the next chapter of your life. It's you who will write every new chapter from now on, and no one else will dictate it to you. It's you, and no one else.

No woman is born strong; she builds her strength through the storms she survives. I will write this chapter as beautifully as I can, and I promise—cross my heart—that its beauty will not only serve me, but others too.

The NEXT CHAPTER of my life has just begun, and it must be worth the risk I took for it.

The End

Next chapter of my boat mates in Australia

All of us in the family group, along with some of the singles, left the detention center after a few months. Only Kaviyani and his family had to stay there for over a year. I guess his approach of instilling fear to protect his family didn't work well in that setting.

After one year, they settled in Brisbane, and they are still living there happily. The kids are teenagers now, and thank God they don't remember much about those days.

Meherdad and Lili started living together after they left the detention center, but they broke up a few months later. I never saw Meherdad again, but I heard he married an Asian woman, has four children, and runs his own business in Sydney.

Azar, the chubby girl, and her husband separated after two years of living in Melbourne. Her husband remarried an Australian woman, and they now have a beautiful daughter. Azar started a new relationship, and I heard she is working as a nurse. She cut off contact with us after her divorce.

Reza and Sherri, after many years of trying, were finally blessed with a beautiful baby girl. Reza now runs a very successful painting business in Melbourne.

Lili met a wealthy Iranian tourist from the USA, and now she is married and living in California.

Razi owns a mechanic shop in Sunshine. His mother, after six months, decided to return to Iran to be with her husband, and she forced Gelareh to come back with her. Since being released from the detention center, Gelareh had really begun to appreciate the freedom she had here as a woman. She couldn't convince her mother to stay, and they returned.

Soon after, she married her boyfriend, but she still tells me, whenever we chat on social media, that she wishes she could come back. A few months after they returned, her mother found out that her husband had remarried during her absence. Under Islamic marriage law, a man is allowed to marry up to four wives at the same time. That was how, after decades of marriage, they too separated. Unfortunately, he died two years ago from a heart attack.

Arya started his own business in cabinet making and now runs a very successful business in Melbourne.

Ahmed, the mechanic, and his wife, along with another young couple from that villa—Zara and her husband—left Indonesia weeks after we headed to the ocean. They all arrived on Christmas Island after July 19th, 2013, when the new rules for asylum seekers came into effect: none of the newly arrived asylum seekers would be able to settle in Australia permanently. Because of this, all of them had to spend long periods—some even years—in detention centers.

Ahmed Tara, and their son were freed from detention after almost two years, just when Tara became pregnant. They were released into the community, and now Ahmed runs a successful mechanic shop in Melbourne, and they have a beautiful daughter.

The girls also had to stay in detention for some time, but Rema and her daughter were released soon because she was pregnant. Fariba, however, ended up on Nauru for a long time. Finally, after spending years in detention, she was released into the community. She is now married and has two beautiful daughters.

Mahdi also ended up spending a long time on Nauru and Christmas Island. Eventually, he was released into the community and now runs his own barber shop in Springfield, Melbourne. He is about 25 years old now.

The athletic boy is a fitness coach in Melbourne. He is married and has a daughter. Every time I see him, the first thing he says is, "Mrs. Zartabi, why did you ruin our lives?" And then we both laugh.

Among us, it was Mohamad and Zara who had the longest time in detention—over seven years in Nauru and other centers. They were finally released, but they were both devastated and depressed from the experience. They are now doing their best to forget the dark memories of those years. Zara is a successful carer, and Mohammad works in community services. They are expecting their first child soon—perhaps by the time this book is published, their son will be born as an Australian citizen.

As for me, I didn't just let my experience on the boat go to waste; I've tried to help others as much as I can. From the day I arrived at the detention center until now, I have been doing everything possible to serve and assist asylum seekers and refugees. It's all on a volunteer basis, as I don't have an official academic certificate for interpreting and translating, so it can't be a paid job.

In 2014, I established a non-profit organization with the same name on social media: *House of Asylum Seekers*. We work in partnership with various other organizations, providing any kind of assistance we can to refugees, asylum seekers, and newly arrived migrants. As for my paid job, I run cooking classes, teaching Australians about Iranian cuisine, culture, and history. I also use my passion for cooking to raise awareness about refugees, asylum seekers, and those bravely fighting for a better Iran in the near future.

I received my permanent residency in June 2023, a milestone that should have marked a fresh start. I was looking forward to the chance to finally have my only son by my side after 11 long years apart. But before I could embrace this long-awaited moment, tragedy struck—he lost his life that same year. The permanent residency I had fought so hard for felt like bitter, cold coffee on a snowy day, offering neither warmth nor comfort to my heart and soul.

Special thanks to Rana Ebrahimi for beautifully editing this book and ParisPictures.com for the photo shoot of I & Mahdi.